LEGENDARY
HEROES

LEGENDARY HEROES

EPIC CHARACTERS FROM ACROSS THE AGES

Project Editors Kathakali Banerjee,
Upamanyu Das, Bipasha Roy
Project Art Editors Noopur Dalal, Heena Sharma
Editorial Team Aashirwad Jain, Deeksha Micek,
Shahid Qureshi, Zarak Rais, Nandini Tripathy
Illustrators Sanya Jain, Aparajita Sen,
Diya Varma, Mohd Zishan
Consulting Editor Camilla Hallinan
Senior Picture Researcher Deepak Negi
Deputy Manager, Picture Research Virien Chopra
Deputy Managing Editor Sreshtha Bhattacharya
Deputy Managing Art Editor Shreya Anand
Managing Editor Kingshuk Ghoshal
Managing Art Editor Govind Mittal
Pre-Production Designer Dheeraj Singh
Pre-Production Coordinator Vishal Bhatia
Pre-Production Image Editor Syed Md Farhan
Production Editor Becky Fallowfield
Production Controller John Casey
Jacket Designer Noopur Dalal
DK Delhi Creative Head Malavika Talukder
Publisher Andrew Macintyre
Art Director Mabel Chan

Contributors Andrea Mills, Lizzie Munsey
Lead Consultant Nathan Robert Brown
Consultants Pearl Brower, Manuel May Castillo,
Mary-Alice Daniel, Hammad Rind, Pavel Horák,
Aziza Ibrokhimova, Salima Ikram, Carolyne Larrington,
Ragnhild Ljosland, Andrew Ng Hock Soon,
David Stuttard, Timothy Topper
Sensitivity Reader Sarosh Arif
Fact Checker Steve Hoffman

First published in Great Britain in 2025 by
Dorling Kindersley Limited
20 Vauxhall Bridge Road,
London, SW1V 2SA

The authorised representative in the EEA is
Dorling Kindersley Verlag GmbH. Arnulfstr. 124,
80636 Munich, Germany

Copyright © 2025 Dorling Kindersley Limited
A Penguin Random House Company
10 9 8 7 6 5 4 3 2 1
001–344482–Jul/2025

A CIP catalogue record for this book
is available from the British Library.
ISBN: 978-0-2417-1128-6

Printed and bound in China

www.dk.com

This book was made with Forest
Stewardship Council™ certified
paper – one small step in DK's
commitment to a sustainable future.
Learn more at www.dk.com/uk/
information/sustainability

CONTENTS

FORMIDABLE WARRIORS 40

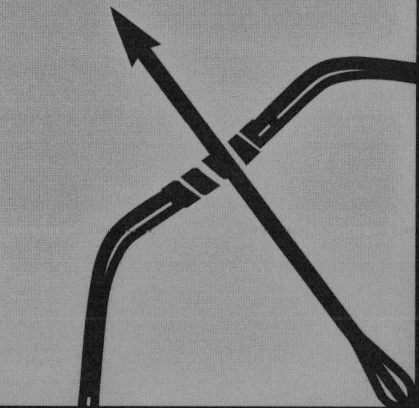

INCLUDING EVERYONE

A team of editors, designers, and experts from different nations, cultures, communities, heritages, and experiences have come together to make this book, using lots of lenses and viewpoints in their work. In this book, we have tried to be global in coverage and inclusive in our contents. We have also done our best to be respectful when referring to any figures that come from various belief systems.

INDIGENOUS HEROES

This book features some Indigenous heroes. Their stories have been written with help from Indigenous experts.

SACRED STORIES

This book includes sacred stories from some cultures.

LEGENDARY HEROES

Legends are stories from the past that have become a lasting part of a people's culture. These traditional tales may be fantastical, but they describe events or deeds that teach important lessons to inspire people. At the heart of these legendary stories are characters with exceptional qualities, sometimes of semi-divine origins, who have become heroes by overcoming obstacles, braving epic journeys, slaying monsters, or saving their people. Classic versions of these stories are adapted and retold over time, and their appeal endures in the modern world where legendary heroes are still celebrated to this day.

HOW DO LEGENDS GROW?

Legends typically begin by word of mouth. These oral tales spread between communities, growing larger than life. Many legends are then recorded in manuscripts, epic poems, folktales, storybooks, plays, and films, helping them to be passed down from one generation to the next.

WHAT MAKES A HERO

Heroes are defined by certain qualities or characteristics that they may have in abundance. Some heroes embody only one quality, while others display many of them. Which traits a culture or people considers heroic may vary around the world.

VALOUR
Heroes face danger head on, showing immense courage or valour. Whether fighting on the battlefield or slaying a monster, they embrace all challenges, just like Lancelot, a knight of King Arthur's court.

STRENGTH
Physical strength is a common trait in legendary heroes, enabling them to defeat almost any opponent and achieve impossible tasks. In Greek mythology, Heracles displays superhuman strength.

INTELLIGENCE
Many heroes succeed using their cleverness and quick-thinking, escaping danger or outwitting foes and rivals. This is how the Greek hero Odysseus avoided countless perils during his epic voyage.

COMPASSION
Some heroes show deep concern for people who are suffering. This natural empathy makes them put others first. The Hindu hero Yudhishthira looked out for everyone, from his beloved family to complete strangers.

A HELPING HAND
While heroes often find themselves facing danger, they aren't always alone. Help can take different forms, such as friends and allies, animal companions, gifts of exceptional weaponry, or the kindness of strangers. The Persian hero Rostam relied on his trusty steed Rakhsh to help fight his foes.

ROSTAM (FAR LEFT) BATTLES ESFANDIYĀR

SUPERNATURAL SKILLS
Some heroes are born with magical powers or given extraordinary capabilities by the gods. Medea's powers of sorcery came from her grandfather, the Sun god Helios.

ANGABO SLAYS ARWE

UNLIKELY HEROES

It is not always the strongest and cleverest who become legendary heroes. The most unexpected ordinary individuals can rise to a challenge, fuelled by determination and the will to protect innocent people. The Ethiopian peasant Angabo's slaying of the monstrous serpent Arwe turned him into a legend.

Tomoe Gozen was an excellent horse rider who could even tame wild horses.

DETERMINATION
Heroes never give up, displaying a dogged determination to achieve their goals. American folk hero John Henry lost his life in his quest to prove that people were more powerful than a steam drill.

LEADERSHIP
Strong leadership skills can make all the difference in bloodthirsty battles or on arduous journeys. Uplifting goals and guidance inspire others to succeed. The British warrior-queen Boudicca's leadership inspired her army in their fight for freedom.

LOYALTY
Even in the face of great adversity, heroes remain loyal to their comrades, leaders, or loved ones. This unwavering support reinforces their strength. Japanese warrior Tomoe Gozen was loyal to her samurai lord to the end.

UNCOMMON ORIGINS

Many heroes are human, but there are others whose true origins are shrouded in mystery. They may have descended from the gods, making them demigods (beings with one divine parent) in some cultures. They often possess supernatural abilities not seen in ordinary people. The ancient Greek demigod Perseus could only slay the gorgon Medusa with gifts from the gods.

WHY DO WE NEED A HERO?
Heroes are important. Throughout history and across cultures, their bravery, determination, and resilience have been a source of hope and inspiration, motivating ordinary people to succeed in their own lives and battle through troubled times. Legendary heroes are enduring role models who prove that even the toughest obstacle can be overcome. And everyone loves a good story – some involve comical trickery or end in tragedy, but these inspiring tales are always thrilling.

FOUNDERS AND RULERS

Many legendary heroes were great leaders who ruled kingdoms, expanded territories, and established empires around the world. In pursuit of power and glory, they built cities, founded civilizations, embraced progress, and laid the foundations for future generations to follow in their footsteps.

ROMULUS
FOUNDER OF ROME

Against all odds, driven and determined Romulus built the ancient city of Rome and crowned himself its first king.

Romulus had come a long way from the troubles of his childhood. When Romulus and his twin brother Remus were babies, they were abandoned on the banks of the River Tiber by their great-uncle, King Amulius, who believed that the children would one day take his throne. Miraculously, they survived, and were raised by a she-wolf. When the brothers grew up, they worked together to overthrow their great-uncle, but a later quarrel between the two ended with Romulus killing Remus. He went on to found Rome, which would become one of the world's most powerful cities.

The great Trojan hero **Aeneas** was an ancestor of Romulus.

KNOW YOUR HERO

Romulus and Remus's struggles are at the heart of the foundation myth of ancient Rome and its vast empire.

Romulus was the son of the god of war, Mars, and a mortal woman called Rhea Silvia. His name is forever linked to Rome.

Legend has it that Romulus founded the city of Rome in 753 BCE and became its first ruler. He ruled for nearly 40 years.

RAISED BY A WOLF
When a she-wolf found Romulus and Remus on the banks of the River Tiber, she raised them as her own. The twins drink her milk in this bronze sculpture.

BUILDING ROME
Romulus supervises the construction of his new city in this Italian ceramic plate from the 19th century. He named the new settlement Roma. The city of Rome would become the beating heart of the vast Roman Empire, and it is still the capital of Italy today.

Romulus threw a spear at Remus, fatally wounding him.

SIBLING RIVALRY
Romulus and Remus were competitive brothers. When they decided to set up a new city, they argued about the exact location. When Romulus began building a city wall, Remus mocked its height by jumping over it. Romulus took revenge by killing his twin.

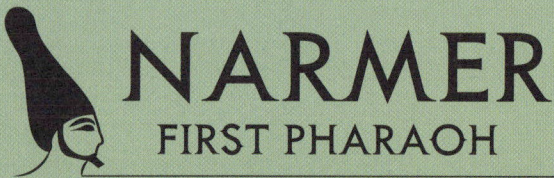

NARMER
FIRST PHARAOH

The pharaoh (king) of Egypt, Narmer, changed the course of his country's history by uniting two warring kingdoms.

Around 5,000 years ago, the northern kingdom of Lower Egypt was at war with the southern kingdom of Upper Egypt. A ruthless warrior, Narmer ushered in an era of peace by bringing these kingdoms together, creating the country's First Dynasty. Under his rule, the people flourished in a time of prosperity, which saw the birth of great cities, including the capital at Memphis.

KNOW YOUR HERO

 The legend of Narmer was first mentioned by Manetho, an ancient Egyptian historian, in the 3rd century BCE.

 Pharaoh Narmer ruled Egypt during the Early Dynastic Period after unifying two opposing kingdoms into one nation.

 He is famous for being the first king of a unified Egypt, founding the First Dynasty of pharaohs in around 3150 BCE.

According to some historians, Narmer was killed by a **hippo.**

The king is about to strike down an enemy with his war club.

A sandal-bearer carries Narmer's sandals, symbol of his power over the earth he walked on.

PALETTE OF VICTORY

Known as the Narmer Palette, this stone tablet was engraved about 3,000 years ago, and was discovered in an Egyptian temple in 1898. It shows King Narmer wearing the crown of Upper Egypt as he conquers Lower Egypt, watched by the falcon-god Horus.

THESEUS
MINOTAUR'S DOOM

The Greek hero Theseus faced countless challenges, but the ultimate showdown was his slaying of the half-man, half-bull Minotaur in the labyrinth.

When King Minos of Crete demanded that the kingdom of Athens send seven young men and seven young women as a sacrifice to the Minotaur every nine years, Theseus journeyed to Crete to get rid of the monster for good. His mission would have been impossible without Princess Ariadne's help – she told him how to navigate the labyrinth and return without losing his way. Theseus took on the beast in a ferocious battle to the death and won. On his triumphant return to Athens, he was crowned king.

MONSTER SLAYER
King Minos of Crete kept the monstrous Minotaur imprisoned inside a great maze, called a labyrinth. Theseus successfully navigated this maze before slaying the monster with his sword, as depicted on this 6th-century BCE vessel from ancient Greece.

ARIADNE'S THREAD
Theseus avoided getting lost in the labyrinth thanks to Ariadne, daughter of King Minos. As shown above, she fell in love with Theseus and gave him a thread to unravel as he walked through the maze so that he could find his way back again.

KNOW YOUR HERO

The story of Theseus and the Minotaur is set in the Minoan civilization of Crete that flourished in c.2000 BCE.

Theseus was an epic Greek hero and an early king of Athens, where his long reign brought peace.

Theseus's life was packed with adventure, but his name is forever linked with the slaying of the Minotaur.

ANAWRAHTA MINSAW
MONARCH OF MYANMAR

A prince of a small kingdom who saw a meteoric rise to the top, Anawrahta Minsaw founded the mighty Pagan Empire. Anawrahta defeated his stepbrother in single combat to take the throne of the kingdom of Pagan. Once he became king, he built canals to improve agriculture, made his military stronger, and turned Pagan into a powerful state. Over the next ten years, he conquered nearby kingdoms, creating the Pagan Empire, which ultimately became modern-day Myanmar.

Anawrahta was introduced to Buddhism by a monk named **Shin Arahan.**

A KING'S LEGACY
King Anawrahta was the first temple builder of Bagan, Pagan's capital city, where thousands of Buddhist temples still stand today. His legacy can also be seen in theatre dramas on his life, as well as the statues and plaques that bear his name.

KNOW YOUR HERO

According to local chronicles, Anawrahta reigned in the 11th century CE and converted to Buddhism in 1056 CE.

The prince of a small kingdom, Anawrahta became the father of the modern-day nation of Myanmar.

Anawrahta is famous for founding the mighty Pagan Empire, which lasted until 1287 CE.

HIAWATHA
GENTLE PEACEMAKER

The Indigenous Onondaga hero Hiawatha brought lasting peace to a troubled region.

During the 16th century, the Indigenous nations around modern-day New York, US, were at war with each other. Hiawatha, leader of the Onondaga people, and the Mohawk leader Dekanawidah, met the chiefs of the other nations and suggested a pact to end the conflict and unite against invaders. The result was the Haudenosaunee Confederacy (originally a union of five nations), which still stands today.

KNOW YOUR HERO

 Hiawatha's stories have been passed down from generation to generation over centuries.

 He was a wise chief of the Onondaga people, and a skilful speaker who could bring people together.

 He is known for forging lasting peace between five Indigenous nations.

Replica of the Hiawatha Belt

BELT OF PEACE
The Haudenosaunee people handcrafted wampum beads from clam shells. Belts created by stringing together these beads were used to mark agreements. The Hiawatha Belt represented the peace agreement between the Cayuga, Mohawk, Oneida, Onondaga, and Seneca peoples.

PEACEKEEPER
It is believed the Onondaga chief smoked a pipe to inform everyone that he wished to discuss peace. In reality, Hiawatha probably travelled between the warring sides and spoke to them to stop the fighting.

Peace pipe

Snakes were sacred creatures representing wisdom and protection.

ÑAIMLAP
DIVINE VOYAGER

Long ago, before the time of the Incas, the legendary sailor Ñaimlap landed on the shores of Peru and founded the prehistoric kingdom of Sicán.

Although Ñaimlap's exact origins are unknown, he arrived at Peru's northern coast with his wife and 40 officials. Sicán, which meant "temple of the Moon", flourished under his rule. His people admired him so much that they started to think he had divine powers. They believe that he sprouted wings and flew away when he died – taking a final flight to the afterlife.

ARRIVAL BY SEA
Ñaimlap sailed to Peru on a traditional boat made from woven reeds of the totora bulrush plant, as seen in this painting by Peruvian artist Ricardo Inga Arizola. While some legends say he was a sailor, others describe him as a deity who appeared unexpectedly on the water.

CEREMONIAL KNIVES
Peruvian rulers typically carried ornate ceremonial knives known as *tumi*, featuring images of heroes and deities. Skilled metalworkers handcrafted these knives, which were used in rituals and ceremonies. This one shows Ñaimlap wearing a headdress in hammered gold and turquoise.

KNOW YOUR HERO

Ñaimlap's legends come from the northern coast of Peru and date back to the 8th century CE.

A fair and just king, Ñaimlap was given divine status by the people of Sicán.

Ñaimlap is known for his seafaring skills and successful governance over the Lambayeque region.

The "Ñaim" in Ñaimlap means "bird" in a Peruvian language called Mochica.

FEATHERED DEITY
Archaeologists have discovered multiple tombs and a temple at Chotuna-Chornancap, the ceremonial heart of Sicán culture. Vivid murals painted on the walls between the 8th and 13th centuries CE pay homage to Ñaimlap. This example shows him as a birdlike deity. In some stories, he was buried under the pyramid at Chotuna, but his tomb has yet to be found.

Birdlike crest, wings, and beak

INCA ROYALTY
Manco Cápac is a glorious Inca emperor adorned in valuable gold in this late 18th-century Peruvian oil painting.

Cápac's cloak is intricately embroidered.

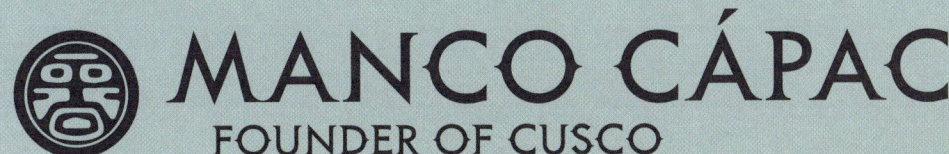

MANCO CÁPAC
FOUNDER OF CUSCO

Guided by the Sun god, Inti, Manco Cápac founded the city of Cusco and became its first ruler.

When Inti saw that the people on Earth were not flourishing, he sent his seven children, including Manco Cápac, to Earth to guide human civilization. Cápac chose the site for a new city by sticking his golden staff into the ground – where the staff sank completely, the land was fertile. He gathered people there and taught them important life skills, such as how to build houses, make tools, and farm. He called the city Cusco. It flourished under his able rule, growing into the centre of the mighty Inca civilization.

MAMA OCLLO
In some versions of the story, Manco Cápac's wife, Mama Ocllo, was the daughter of the Moon goddess, Mama Kilya. She taught Inca women how to spin thread and then weave it into fabric.

KNOW YOUR HERO

Inca legends of Manco Cápac date back to 13th-century Peru.

Manco Cápac was the son of the Inca Sun deity, and grew up to be a great leader of his people.

He established the Inca civilization at Cusco.

CITIES OF LEGEND
The city of Cusco (seen below) was set up in the 13th century CE and is one of the longest-inhabited cities in the Americas. Many other legendary cities are still flourishing today, such as Luxor in Egypt and Kyoto in Japan.

GOLDEN SUN
Inti was the most powerful of all Inca deities. Farmers prayed to Inti for plentiful harvests, and the Inca built impressive temples to honour him. This mask from Ecuador shows Inti in solid gold. Inca artists often depicted rays of golden light streaming from his head.

KRISHNA

An avatar of the Hindu God Vishnu, blue-skinned Krishna is the deity of love, kindness, and protection. He gave advice to the hero Arjuna during the Kurukshetra War (see p.82). When Arjuna was unsure of fighting his own family members in the war, Krishna convinced the hero to do his duty as a warrior.

Aengus is often shown with birds flocking around his head.

AENGUS

Handsome Aengus is the Celtic god of love. He helped lovers in trouble, such as the warrior Diarmuid (see p.77). This hero fell in love with a princess who was engaged to someone else, so the pair went on the run. Aengus gave Diarmuid a deadly sword, guided the couple along safe paths, and protected the princess with his cloak of invisibility.

HELPFUL DEITIES

Gods and goddesses play a central role in many myths, legends, and sacred stories from around the world. They often lend heroes their support. Sometimes, heroes receive aid from a deity when they need it the most. Gods and goddesses may raise abandoned babies, warn of impending dangers, grant special abilities, or give generous gifts, such as magical objects or weapons. But jealous or competitive deities may not help at all – instead, they may choose to make it harder for a hero to reach their goals.

HEPHAESTUS

Hephaestus was the ancient Greek god of fire. A skilled blacksmith, he forged a shield and suit of armour for the warrior Achilles during the Trojan War (see p.58). He gave them to Achilles' mother, the sea goddess Thetis, to take to the hero, as seen in this Greek vase painting from around 480 BCE.

Ancient Greek gods often had children with humans, creating **demigods.**

ENKI

The ancient Mesopotamian god Enki was the creator of humanity. He warned the hero Atrahasis that the world was about to be overwhelmed by a great flood. This gave Atrahasis time to build an ark to save himself and two of every kind of animal in the world.

ATHENA

The ancient Greek war goddess Athena often involved herself in the adventures of heroes, sharing gifts and advice with those she favoured. Her mirrored shield (right) let the hero Perseus defeat the gorgon Medusa (see p.45). Athena also helped Heracles during his 12 labours – she lent him her divine strength to hold up the sky (see p.51) while the Titan god Atlas went to fetch the magical apples of the Hesperides.

HINA

The Polynesian moon goddess Hina guided and supported the hero Māui. She taught him to plait her hair into a rope, which he used to capture the Sun (see p.134). In one tale, she carried Māui's fishhook deep into the ocean, helping him reel in the islands of Hawai'i.

DIDO
CLEVER QUEEN

Princess Dido fled her troubled past to find a future ruling her own kingdom in Africa. Dido married a wealthy priest named Acerbas. When her greedy brother Pygmalion killed Acerbas to steal his hidden treasures, Dido searched out her husband's loot, gathered followers, and sailed across the Mediterranean Sea to Africa. There, she used her wits to found the great city of Carthage (in modern-day Tunisia) and crowned herself queen.

Dido was born in the city of Tyre, in present-day Lebanon.

MINTED MONARCH
Dido established Carthage on a great hill overlooking the Mediterranean Sea, and it prospered under her rule. She featured on local coins, such as this one minted in Carthage in the 4th century BCE but found in Sicily.

KNOW YOUR HERO

 Dido appears in ancient Greek and Roman works from the 3rd century BCE onwards – most famously in the *Aeneid* by the Roman poet Virgil.

 Daughter of the Phoenician king Mutto of Tyre, Dido was renowned for her wit and wisdom.

 Dido received the land she needed by clever means, and used it to create one of the most successful cities in ancient history.

BULL BOUNDARY
When Dido arrived in North Africa, a local chieftain named Iarbas declared she could only buy any land encompassed by a bull's hide. As shown in this 17th-century engraving, Dido cunningly asked that the hide be cut into fine strips, giving her enough to mark out a large area for Carthage. According to legend, Dido founded her new city in 814 BCE.

LONDINIUM BURNING

Boudicca and her army raged across the country, sacking Roman towns and military outposts. Thousands fled or died when she sacked the new Roman settlement at Londinium (present-day London) and set it alight, as seen in this early 19th-century engraving.

FEARLESS LEADER

Brutally mistreated by the Romans, Boudicca refused to be cowed. Leading her army from a horse-drawn chariot with spear in hand, she is shown in all her glory in this 19th-century bronze sculpture by British artist Thomas Thornycroft in London.

BOUDICCA
BLAZING REBEL

Brave Boudicca was a woman on a mission, unleashing her fighting spirit to lead a struggle for independence. Boudicca's husband was the king of the Iceni tribe in ancient Britain. After his death, Roman invaders took over their land, so the fierce queen led her tribe in a great rebellion. Although it ultimately failed, her army destroyed many major Roman settlements, almost stopping the Roman colonization of Britain.

KNOW YOUR HERO

The tale of Queen Boudicca was first recorded by the Roman historian Tacitus in c.98 CE and 110 CE.

The queen of the Iceni tribe remains a national hero in Britain.

She is best known for spearheading a revolt against the Romans in c.60 CE.

SERPENT SLAYER
Ragnar won the hand of his wife Thora by killing the giant serpent that guarded her quarters. To protect himself from the snake's deadly venom, he wore thick woollen breeches smeared with tar – as shown in this 1899 illustration by British artist Henry Justice Ford – and earned the name Lothbrok ("shaggy breeches") for his attire.

KNOW YOUR HERO

Tales of Ragnar Lothbrok were first written down in Iceland during the 12th century.

This Viking (Old Norse) hero was a warrior king whose deeds became known across medieval Europe.

He is best known for slaying a deadly serpent and for his sons, who became renowned warriors.

RAGNAR LOTHBROK
VIKING RAIDER

One name sure to strike fear in enemy hearts was that of Viking warrior Ragnar Lothbrok.

A legendary hero in the Norse sagas, Ragnar had a meteoric rise to the throne. In one version of his story, he led armies in a series of devastating raids across the British Isles in the 8th–9th centuries CE and was crowned king of Denmark and Sweden.

VIKING EXPLORERS
From the 8th century CE, many farmers from Denmark, Norway, and Sweden left their homeland to explore and expand their territory. Famous Viking explorer Leif Erikson, immortalized in bronze in this statue in Reykjavik, Iceland, was the first European to reach the continent that would be called North America, around the year 1000 CE.

LUGH
GLORIOUS LEADER

A hero with exceptional talents, Lugh ushered ancient Ireland into an era of peace and prosperity.

The Celtic warrior Lugh was a master craftsman, poet, magician, and athlete. Legend has it that he became the leader of his clan of warrior-gods, the Tuatha Dé Danann, by performing three feats: winning a throwing competition, impressing his people by playing the harp, and defeating the clan's king in a board game known as fidchell. With spear in hand, Lugh led his clan to victory in the great Battle of Mag Tuired against the rival Fomorians, and was crowned the new High King of Ireland.

KNOW YOUR HERO

Stories featuring this figure from Irish oral lore were first written down in the 11th-century manuscript *Cath Maige Tuired* ("The Battle of Mag Tuired").

Lugh is a supernatural hero, as dazzling as the Sun, and blessed with godly abilities and the valour of a warrior.

He is well known for winning the Battle of Mag Tuired and ruling Ireland for 40 years. His son was the legendary warrior Cú Chulainn.

Lugh's name is preserved in the Irish harvest festival **Lughnasa.**

Lugh's magical fiery spear, called Gáe Assail, was one of the four most important treasures of the Tuatha Dé Danann.

GRAND VICTORY
The leader of the Fomorians was Lugh's grandfather, a giant named Balor of the Evil Eye. At the Battle of Mag Tuired, Lugh killed Balor by driving a spear through his eye, as shown on this commemorative coin from modern-day Ireland.

GILGAMESH
MIGHTY OVERLORD

ISHTAR'S WRATH
This clay figure from c.1500 BCE shows Ishtar, the ancient Mesopotamian goddess of love. She fell in love with Gilgamesh and wanted to marry him, but when he refused her offer, the enraged goddess unleashed a bull to punish him.

Part god, part human, Gilgamesh ruled over the city of Uruk in ancient Mesopotamia, way back in c.27th century BCE. Gilgamesh's knowledge and strength made him an arrogant ruler, so the gods sent Enkidu to teach him a lesson about humanity. Enkidu challenged Gilgamesh to a fight, but they were too evenly matched – after fighting for hours, they declared a truce and became friends. The pair defeated every challenge the gods sent Gilgamesh's way, angering them so much that the gods decided to kill Enkidu. Gilgamesh was terrified that he too would die, so he travelled to the underworld to find a way to cheat death, but he failed. Accepting that everyone must die, he returned to Uruk a wiser king.

KNOW YOUR HERO

Gilgamesh is the hero of the ancient Mesopotamian poem, the *Epic of Gilgamesh*, which is around 4,000 years old.

This demigod was a warrior-king of Uruk, a city in Mesopotamia (present-day Iraq).

Gilgamesh defeated many monsters and journeyed to the underworld in search of immortality.

Gilgamesh stabs the bull with his sword.

Gilgamesh ruled the city of Uruk for 126 years.

DANGEROUS BEAST
Ishtar's bull was terrifying – just one of its snorts could open a hole in the ground that could swallow 100 people. After a fierce fight, Gilgamesh had to grab the bull by a horn for his fatal blow.

HUANGDI
WISE EMPEROR

China's legendary leader Huangdi was a great warrior, famous for his battle skills.

Huangdi defeated numerous neighbouring tribes, bringing them together to begin the Chinese civilization, and declared himself emperor. He is also known as the creator of many inventions, including the first wooden houses, boats, carts, writing, the bow and arrow, and the game of cuju.

PLAYING CUJU
Huangdi invented cuju, a football-like game that has been played in China for more than 2,000 years. He used it to train his army, so they could get fit and fast by kicking a ball around. Cuju is still played in China today during festivals.

Huangdi is said to have ruled China for exactly 100 years.

Huangdi chats with Lei Gong in his court in this 16th-century illustration.

Huangdi

TEACHING MEDICINE
Huangdi taught his people about medicine. One of the most important ancient Chinese books on medicine, *Huangdi Neijing*, is written as a conversation between Huangdi and his doctor Lei Gong.

Lei Gong

KNOW YOUR HERO

Huangdi is first mentioned in Chinese inscriptions from the 4th century BCE. He is said to have lived more than 4,000 years ago.

He is famous as one of the mythical emperors of China – a great ruler who may never have existed.

Huangdi's rule brought peace and stability to China. His remarkable inventions helped his people to prosper.

JIMMU
ULTIMATE UNIFIER

Japan's legendary first emperor was Jimmu, a descendent of Amaterasu, the Sun goddess. Amaterasu aided Jimmu in his mission to unite Japan, guiding him with the help of a three-legged crow called Yatagarasu. From his village Takachiho in western Japan, he marched with his army to the east, conquering new territories and uniting rival clans. Whether he was a historical ruler or a legend remains a mystery, but his story marks the beginning of the imperial dynasty and great nation of Japan.

The white circle represents the Jewel.

Kusanagi
no Tsurugi
(The Sword)

Yasakani no
Magatama
(The Jewel)

Yata no
Kagami
(The Mirror)

SACRED TREASURES
Legend has it that goddess Amaterasu visited Jimmu in a vision and predicted that he would one day lead Japan. She gave him three sacred treasures – a sword, a jewel, and a mirror. Shown here in an illustration from an 18th-century scroll, they are still the most important royal treasures in Japan.

KNOW YOUR HERO

Emperor Jimmu first appears in 8th-century Japanese texts – the *Kojiki* and *Nihon Shoki*.

While he may be a legendary figure from Japan's past, some parts of his story are based on true events.

Jimmu is celebrated as the first emperor of Japan, coming to power on 11 February in 660 BCE.

Emperor Jimmu

EASTERN EXPEDITION
Armed with his great bow, Jimmu is shown with kneeling warriors in this woodblock print by Japanese artist Adachi Ginkō. When his forces reached Yamato in eastern Japan, Jimmu was crowned emperor there and ruled Japan until he died at the age of 126.

Japan's National Foundation Day falls on 11 February.

DRAGONFLY ISLANDS
In the *Kojiki*, a book of Japanese legends, Japan was called Akitsushima, which means "Dragonfly Islands". Emperor Jimmu once stood on top of a mountain and looked down at Japan's chain of islands, likening their shape to a pair of dragonflies.

DARING LEADER
During Zenobia's uprising against Rome, she captured the provinces of Asia Minor (a region in modern-day Turkey/Türkiye) and Egypt, becoming a powerful symbol of rebellion against Roman rule. She was very popular, and her likeness appeared on many objects, such as this copper coin minted in Egypt around 271 CE.

KNOW YOUR HERO

Zenobia was a historical figure from Syria, whose details were recorded by ancient Roman historians.

An intelligent and capable ruler, she ruled Palmyra in present-day Syria from c.267 to 272 CE.

Famous for rebelling against Roman rule, she is still a patriotic symbol in Syria today.

Zenobia leads her forces in defending her city.

SEPTIMIA ZENOBIA
FREEDOM FIGHTER

Queen of Palmyra, Septimia Zenobia was brave enough to fight back against the might of the Roman Empire.

After her husband was killed, Zenobia began ruling the Roman colony of Palmyra (in modern-day Syria) as regent for her son. A formidable leader known for her intelligence, Zenobia was not happy under Rome's control, so she fought to declare Palmyra's independence. Under her leadership, it expanded greatly. When the Roman emperor Aurelian came to reclaim the territory, she went toe-to-toe with him, but she was eventually defeated.

DEFENDING PALMYRA
The queen's rebellion came to an end when the city of Palmyra was besieged by the Romans, and the Palmyran forces were defeated. Zenobia attempted to flee the city, but she was captured and taken to Rome as a prisoner.

A GREAT BATTLE
When Heracles stole Hippolyta's girdle, the Amazons attacked Greece, but were defeated by the Athenians led by Theseus. This battle, known as the Amazonomachy, often features in ancient Greek art, such as this stone coffin from the 2nd century CE.

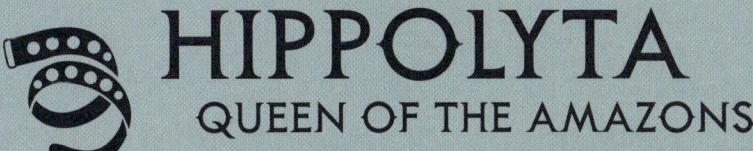

HIPPOLYTA
QUEEN OF THE AMAZONS

The Amazons were mighty warrior women and their leader Hippolyta was the strongest of them all.
Hippolyta and her Amazons appear in the legends of two key Greek heroes: Theseus and Heracles. The Amazons' queen, Hippolyta, was a skilled horse rider, fierce archer, and an exceptional swordswoman. Around her waist Hippolyta wore a particular kind of war belt called a girdle, which had been given to her by her father, Ares, god of war.

Hippolyta means "she who unleashes the horses".

KNOW YOUR HERO

 Hippolyta features in ancient Greek stories, including those in Apollodorus' *Bibliotheca*, a collection of ancient Greek myths from the 2nd century CE.

 She is a legendary warrior queen, famous for her skills in both leadership and fighting.

 Hippolyta is known for leading a tribe of female warriors – the Amazons – and for the magical belt that gave her incredible strength.

LOSING THE GIRDLE
Hippolyta's girdle was stolen from her by the hero Heracles, who was given this task as one of his famous 12 labours (see pp.48–51). Hippolyta and her opponent were both skilled fighters, but in the end, she could not overpower Heracles, who had superhuman strength.

ARTHUR
FABLED MONARCH

Shrouded in magic and mystery, the legendary tales of King Arthur have captured people's imagination for centuries.

Born the son of Uther Pendragon, a legendary king of the Britons at a time of great strife, Arthur was given to the wizard Merlin who had him raised away from the royal family. Arthur grew up to become a brave knight, heroic warrior, and revered leader who won numerous battles and united the people of Britain in the 5th–6th centuries CE. His court at Camelot achieved lasting fame for its chivalry – the medieval code of honour that all knights swore to uphold.

The golden dragon on Arthur's helmet was a symbol of the house of Pendragon.

THE FINAL BATTLE
King Arthur defended his crown when his nephew Mordred tried to overthrow him. In their deadly duel after the Battle of Camlann, each fatally wounded the other. After Arthur's death, his body was taken to the Isle of Avalon.

MAGICAL MENTOR
Saxon armies were a constant threat, so Arthur was given to Merlin as a baby, as seen in this 19th-century bronze sculpture by Welsh artist William Goscombe John. Merlin became Arthur's protector and mentor, educating him when he grew up and guiding him even when he became king.

KNOW YOUR HERO

The History of the Kings of Britain by Welsh writer Geoffrey of Monmouth popularized ancient tales of Arthur.

It's not known whether King Arthur ever existed, but he remains a much-loved folk hero from medieval literature.

He famously pulled the sword from the stone and based his court at Camelot. It became a symbol of medieval chivalry.

Legend has it that Arthur will one day return to **rule again.**

LEGEND RETOLD
Arthur's story has inspired countless retellings in literature, paintings, music, and other art forms, adding new details through the ages. The 2004 film *King Arthur* reimagines him as an officer in the Roman army (seen here as the head of the cavalry).

LEGENDARY SWORD
When Uther died, Merlin placed a sword in an anvil on a stone, declaring that whoever pulled it out would become king. Hundreds of men tried, but only young Arthur succeeded in drawing the sword – as pictured in this 1930s stained-glass window in Tintagel, Cornwall.

KNIGHTS OF THE ROUND TABLE

The distinctive shape of King Arthur's Round Table meant that everyone who sat on it was equal and there was no head of the table. They respected their worthy ruler and vowed to follow a strict code of honour and service to the kingdom. Some of the most memorable knights of the Round Table are introduced here, although legend has it there were many more.

ARTHUR
The king selected the best knights to sit at his famous Round Table. The wizard Merlin helped him decide and also made suggestions of his own. King Arthur led the meetings, which ranged from discussions on military tactics to celebratory feasts.

GALAHAD
The son of Lancelot (see p.74), Galahad was known for his pure heart, strong morals, noble character, and exceptional skills with the sword. He was also one of only three knights to ever find the Holy Grail. (See also Bors, right, and Perceval, pp.112–113.)

KAY
Known as Kay the Tall, this imposing knight was the son of Ector. He was Arthur's adoptive brother and steward – Kay was responsible for testing the skills of new warriors in Camelot.

TRISTAN
A close companion of Arthur, Tristan was an expert hunter and a talented harpist. When tasked with bringing an Irish princess called Iseult to marry his uncle, the King of Cornwall, he broke the knights' code of honour by falling in love with her.

BEDIVERE
Among the first knights at the table, Bedivere was one of Arthur's closest friends. He was known for his enduring bravery and loyalty. Despite losing one hand in battle, he still ranked among the fiercest warriors in Camelot.

More than **150 knights** sat at King Arthur's Round Table.

GAWAIN

Arguably the perfect knight, King Arthur's nephew was a protector of the poor and was second only to Lancelot as a fighter. A 14th-century poem describes how Gawain beheaded the Green Knight only for the knight to put his head back on his body. Gawain nobly agreed to let the Green Knight cut his head off in return. He was spared, but later died after a duel with Lancelot.

BORS DE GANIS

Loyal to the court and devoted to the king, Bors de Ganis was the only knight to survive the quest for the prized Holy Grail and come back to Camelot – Galahad and Perceval died in the Holy Land. When Bors returned to Camelot, he was held in high esteem at the Round Table.

ECTOR

This older knight adopted Arthur as a young boy and shared his care with Merlin. As a result, his loyalty to the king was deep-rooted and unwavering. Despite his age, Ector was determined to prove himself a capable and noble knight.

MORDRED

Arthur's nephew won a place at the Round Table, but brought ruin. Driven by murderous ambition, Mordred eventually overthrew Arthur's rule and mortally wounded the king.

MEDB
FEARLESS RULER

The Celtic queen Medb was a warrior unlike any other in the Ulster Cycle, a celebrated collection of ancient Irish tales. Medb ruled over the kingdom of Connaught with unrelenting ambition. She went to war with the legendary warrior Cú Chulainn of Ulster after setting her sights on a prized bull that symbolized prestige and power. In their epic showdown, known as the Cattle Raid of Cooley, she eventually won the bull.

KNOW YOUR HERO

 Medb is a mythical queen in the Ulster Cycle of stories that were first written down in the 12th century.

 Medb strikes the balance between royal ruler and fearsome warrior, inspiring generations of women to go for glory.

 She is famous for sending her champions to fight Cú Chulainn, and winning a prized bull called Donn Cúailnge.

WARRIOR QUEEN
Queen Medb is both warrior and ruler in this 1911 portrait by US artist Joseph Christian Leyendecker. She was shown battle ready, with weaponry and shield close at hand.

KNOW YOUR HERO

The story of Eight Deer appears in a 15th-century Mixtec manuscript called *Codex Tonindeye*.

He was an expert negotiator and an ambitious ruler with grand plans for greatness in the 11th century CE.

Eight Deer remains a Mixtec hero to this day, celebrated as a powerful warrior and ruler.

Eight Deer founded the city of Tututepec in Mexico.

RECEIVING TRIBUTE
In this scene from the 15th-century *Codex Tonindeye*, also called the *Codex Zouche-Nuttall*, Eight Deer (right) receives tribute and recognition from the ruler Twelve Vulture. Seated on his throne, he has a turquoise nose ring worn only by a king.

EIGHT DEER JAGUAR CLAW
MIXTEC MASTERMIND

Skilled warrior Eight Deer established a mighty Mixtec state, expanding it into a vast territory in southern Mexico.

Although he was not of royal birth, Eight Deer Jaguar Claw became the most powerful ruler of the Mixtec people. He and his allies conquered almost 100 cities during his rule. His military and political conquests have been recorded in eye-catching Mixtec manuscripts.

REVEALING THE PAST
A codex is an ancient manuscript bound together like a book that reveals the history and culture of a civilization or people. Seen below is the *Dresden Codex*, a Maya book from the 11th or 12th centuries CE.

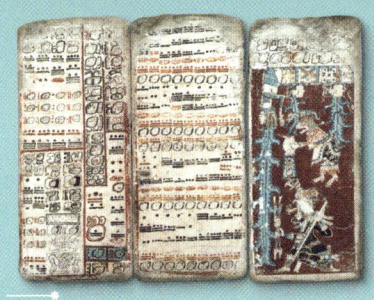

FORMIDABLE WARRIORS

The battlefield brought out the best in the bravest heroes from legend. They fought in many battles, using their strength and skills to devastating effect. Whether waging war against enemy soldiers or slaying monsters, they put their lives on the line to emerge as true champions.

Beowulf raises his sword to strike the final blow.

THE FINAL BATTLE
In his later years, Beowulf battled a fire-breathing dragon that was wreaking havoc throughout his kingdom. This storybook illustration shows their duel to the death. Beowulf, aided by his relative Wiglaf, proved triumphant by killing the dragon with his sword, but the dragon's bite claimed the great hero's life.

KNOW YOUR HERO

With roots in Germany, Britain, and Scandinavia, this hero stars in the Old English epic poem *Beowulf*, written sometime between the 7th and 10th centuries CE.

Beowulf is a classic epic hero, with the typical traits of strength, bravery, and loyalty.

He is best known for his fearless approach to killing the deadliest creatures ever encountered.

19th-century illustration by British artist Henry Matthew Brock

BEOWULF
BEAST SLAYER

The bravest of heroes, Beowulf takes centre stage in an old epic poem as a killer of beasts, from gruesome giants to deadly dragons.

When the Danish people were terrorized by a monstrous ogre named Grendel, a young Beowulf arrived from Geatland (in present-day Sweden) to kill the creature and save them. Beowulf also slayed Grendel's mother when she tried to take revenge. In return, he was rewarded by the Danish king Hrothgar for his courage and heroism. Beowulf returned to his homeland to be crowned King of the Geats, but he was far from finished when it came to slaying monsters!

HROTHGAR'S HALL
Mead halls were places where Norse and Germanic communities gathered to drink mead and feast. Heorot Hall was a great mead hall built by King Hrothgar. Disaster struck when Grendel began killing people at this hall. The giant ogre's menace loomed over Hrothgar's kingdom for 12 years before the hero Beowulf ended his murderous rampage.

A PRICE TO PAY
According to ancient Germanic law, every life had a price. This was known as wergild, meaning "man payment". If a person suffered injuries or death at the hands of another, the culprit had to pay a price, sometimes even with their life. Grendel's mother sought revenge for her son's death because she never received her wergild.

Beowulf is one of the longest surviving Old English poems.

GIANT GRENDEL
Grendel's ferocious appetite resulted in countless victims at Heorot Hall. One day, the monster came to the mead hall, unaware that Beowulf and his men lay in wait. Weapons didn't work against his impenetrable skin and steel-like claws, so Beowulf fought Grendel with his bare hands. When he tore off one of Grendel's arms, the ogre retreated to his cave and died.

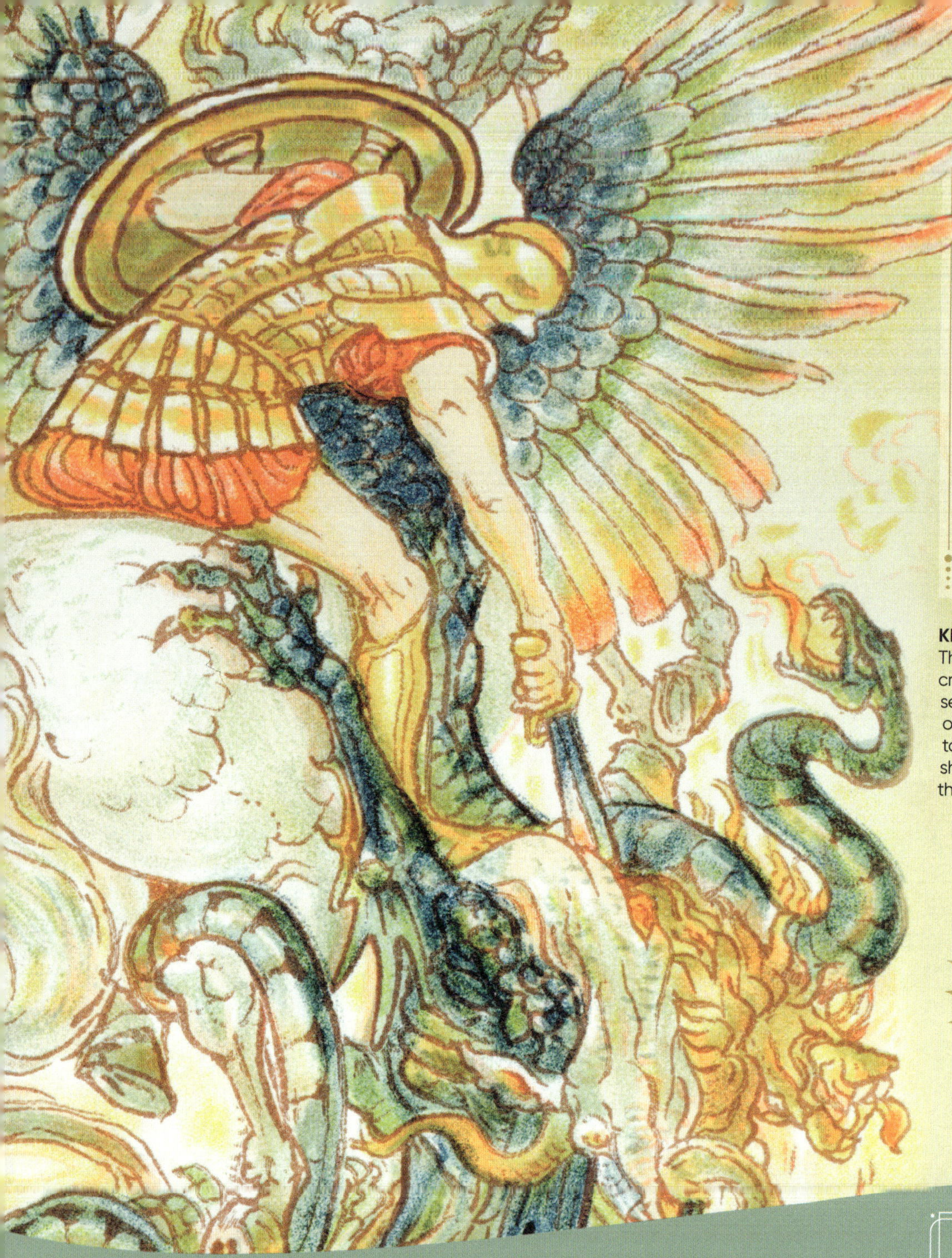

KILLING THE CHIMERA

The fire-breathing Chimera, a monstrous creature with the heads of a lion, goat, and serpent, had begun eating people in the land of Lycia. King Iobates challenged Bellerophon to kill the beast. This 19th-century painting shows the moment when Bellerophon slayed the Chimera with his sword.

Bellerophon used a set of **golden reins** to control Pegasus in flight.

HUBRIS

Excessive arrogance, known as hubris, is always punished by the gods in Greek mythology. When Daedalus made wings for himself and his son Icarus, the boy ignored his father's warning not to fly too close to the Sun – his wings melted away, sending him to his death.

BELLEROPHON
FLYING WARRIOR

The sky was the limit for brave Bellerophon, who rode his winged horse to battle monsters and win wars.

King Iobates of Lycia set multiple challenges for the legendary Greek hero, but Bellerophon proved unstoppable. He and his flying horse Pegasus soared the skies together on countless adventures. When he arrogantly tried galloping to Mount Olympus, the home of the gods, King Zeus sent a gadfly to sting Pegasus – the horse reared in pain, and Bellerophon fell to his death.

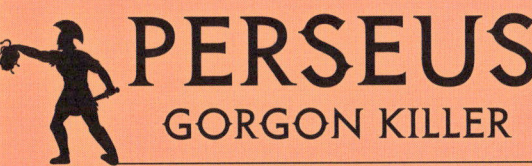

PERSEUS
GORGON KILLER

As the son of Zeus, the king of the gods, Perseus was always destined for greatness.

After falling foul of King Polydectes, Perseus was set the seemingly impossible task of killing the gorgon Medusa, a scaly-skinned, snake-haired monster who turned people to stone with just one look. Aided by the gods, Perseus killed Medusa and used her head to rescue Princess Andromeda from Cetus, an insatiable marine monster.

DEATH OF MEDUSA
How did Perseus avoid the gorgon's deadly gaze? He used a shiny shield given to him by the goddess Athena to look only at Medusa's reflection, and swiftly cut off her head as she slept. Perseus eventually gave Medusa's head to Athena.

16th-century bronze sculpture by Benvenuto Cellini in Florence, Italy

DIVINE ASSISTANCE
Perseus is armed for battle in this Greek vase painting from around 510 BCE. Hades, god of the dead, gave him a cap of invisibility, and the messenger god Hermes gave him a magical sword and winged sandals to fly to Medusa's lair.

KNOW YOUR HERO

 The legend of Perseus comes from ancient Greece, where the poets Homer and Hesiod wrote about him in the 8th century BCE.

 He was a demigod – his parents were the god Zeus and the princess Danaë.

 Perseus is known for slaying the gorgon Medusa and the monstrous sea serpent Cetus.

The ancient Romans knew Heracles as **Hercules.**

TIMELESS LEGEND
The story of Heracles' amazing strength and incredible labours is still popular in modern times. His tale has been told in many different ways, including in books, comics, films, and even a musical.

MIGHTY SAGA OF THE WORLD'S MIGHTIEST MAN !

HERCULES

STEVE REEVES

SYLVA KOSCINA · GIANNA MARIA CANALE

Heracles holds a rock in his raised hand, ready to strike.

Bronze statue of Heracles and Achelous, made in 1824 by French sculptor François-Joseph Bosio

CRISIS IN THE CRADLE
Heracles' first feat of strength was when he was just an infant. The goddess Hera sent two snakes to kill him in his cradle, but baby Heracles strangled them to death.

KNOW YOUR HERO

Heracles was born in the city of Thebes, Greece. His stories date back to 13th–4th centuries BCE.

As a son of the god Zeus and a mortal woman, Alcmene, Heracles was a demigod. He was also a powerful warrior.

Famed for his 12 labours, Heracles is often portrayed wearing the skin of the Nemean Lion and wielding a giant wooden club.

HERACLES
HERO OF HEROES

The slayer of the terrifying Hydra and the tamer of vicious Cerberus, Heracles was a demigod gifted with supernatural strength. Most ancient Greek heroes pale in comparison to him!

Heracles led a life of adventure like no other. His natural strength was obvious from childhood, but he also learned how to wrestle, box, fence, and shoot arrows. Heracles became a hero with both strength and skill, but he had to overcome many obstacles set by the goddess Hera. She hated him because he was her husband Zeus' child with a mortal woman, so she made him lose his mind and murder his family. To atone for his sins, Heracles faced 12 difficult labours.

BATTLING ACHELOUS
Heracles performed incredible feats of strength both before and after his labours. Here he is shown mid-battle with the river god Achelous. Both Heracles and god wanted to marry the princess Deianira, and fought for her hand. Heracles won, despite Achelous switching between the forms of a bull-headed man, snake, and bull.

The river god Achelous in the form of a snake

THE LABOURS OF HERACLES

Mighty Heracles had to take on a series of labours to atone for his wrongdoings. These tasks were imposed on him by Eurystheus, king of the Greek kingdom of Tiryns, who hated Heracles because he was stronger and more famous than him. Each labour was so difficult that it was impossible for an ordinary person to complete, but Heracles used his strength and cunning to overcome task after task.

1 FEROCIOUS LION

Heracles' first task was to kill a fearsome lion, which had been terrorizing the people of Nemea. His arrows could not pierce the beast's golden coat, so Heracles wrestled the lion and strangled it to death with his bare hands. In some versions of the story, he then wore the Nemean Lion's impenetrable coat as armour.

2 HORRIFYING HYDRA

The Hydra was a nine-headed, serpent-like monster that hid in the swampy waters of a place called Lerna. It would emerge from its watery home to eat people and animals. Heracles set out to slay this monster, and was accompanied by his nephew Iolaus in his quest. Heracles sliced off the Hydra's heads one at a time, while Iolaus used fire to stop the heads from growing back.

3 GOLDEN-HORNED DEER

Next, Heracles had to capture the Ceryneian Hind, a huge golden-horned deer that could run faster than a flying arrow. It was sacred to the goddess Artemis, so Heracles did not want to kill or harm the animal. He tracked it for a whole year, waiting for his chance. Eventually, he wounded the deer to catch it by its horns, but Artemis forgave Heracles.

4 BEASTLY BOAR

The next perilous task was to capture the deadly Erymanthian Boar alive. It was a colossal pig with a very bad temper. After a long and tiring chase through the thick snow of Mount Erymanthos, Heracles finally managed to catch the boar. When he carried it back to Eurystheus, the king hid in fear.

Heracles dug trenches to nearby rivers, sending water flowing through the stables.

5 FILTHY STABLES

Heracles' fifth labour was to clean out the famously dirty and smelly stables of King Augeus in a single day. The stables were home to thousands of animals, and they had not been cleaned in 30 years. Shovelling all the poo would take far too long. Instead, Heracles cleverly diverted the waters of nearby rivers through the Augean stables, washing them clean.

6 BOTHERSOME BIRDS

A huge flock of vicious, flesh-eating birds had gathered on a treacherous swamp near Stymphalos, and Heracles was challenged to drive them away. The goddess Athena gave him a set of noise-making clappers, which scared the Stymphalian Birds into the sky so Heracles could shoot them down.

7 MONSTROUS BULL

A fierce bull had been on a rampage through the island of Crete. Its colossal size meant it had left a lot of damage in its wake. Heracles grabbed the Cretan Bull by its horns and slammed it into the ground using his bare hands. Before the bull could recover, Heracles tied it with a rope, and then shipped it back to King Eurystheus in Mycenae.

Heracles had to break the iron chains that kept the horses tied to their troughs.

8 FLESH-EATING MARES

King Diomedes of Thrace owned four wild mares (female horses), which were gigantic and fed on human flesh. Heracles was sent to capture them. In many versions of the story, he killed Diomedes and fed his flesh to his own horses. This calmed the wild beasts and Heracles took them back to Mycenae.

Hippolyta had received her magical belt from her father Ares, the Greek god of war.

9 AMAZONIAN GIRDLE

The Amazons were a tribe of warrior women known for their remarkable skills in hunting and combat. Heracles was tasked with obtaining the magical girdle (belt) of Hippolyta, Queen of the Amazons. Hippolyta fought tooth and nail to protect the girdle, but mighty Heracles overpowered her, stole her belt, and sailed away. In some versions of the story, Heracles had to kill Hippolyta to snatch the belt from her.

10 GIANT'S CATTLE

At the edge of the world in the far west lived a three-bodied giant called Geryon, who kept a herd of red cows. Heracles was sent to steal them and bring them back to Greece. The cattle were guarded by a gigantic hound, Orthrus. Heracles killed Orthrus with a violent blow of his wooden club, and shot Geryon with a poisoned arrow. He then stole the cattle easily, but the journey home was long and hard.

11 GOLDEN APPLES

Heracles was sent to steal three golden apples from the orchard of the Hesperides, the daughters of the Titan god Atlas, who held the sky on his shoulders. Heracles was unable to enter the garden himself, so he asked the god for help. Heracles offered to hold the sky, while Atlas fetched the apples. He then tricked Atlas into taking back the sky and ran away with his prize.

Orthrus's two heads and snakelike tail made him a ferocious guard dog.

The monstrous hound had a mane of fierce snakes.

12 TERRIFYING HOUND

The final task was to capture Cerberus, a three-headed dog that guarded the entrance to the Greek underworld. Here, Heracles met the god Hades, ruler of the underworld. Hades agreed to let Heracles take Cerberus if he could overpower the huge hound without any weapons. Heracles succeeded, thanks to his incredible strength, and took the animal to Mycenae. King Eurystheus was so terrified, he begged Heracles to return Cerberus to the underworld, and promised to end his labours.

ISSUN-BŌSHI
INCH-HIGH SAMURAI

In a Japanese fairytale, being tiny did not stop young Issun-bōshi from being brave.

Issun-bōshi was only an inch tall, but he sought fame and fortune, and managed to sail from his village to a big city armed with only a needle. He became a samurai (Japanese military warrior) tasked with guarding the house of a lord. When an evil ogre kidnapped the lord's daughter, Issun-bōshi attempted to rescue her but was swallowed whole. The brave hero stabbed the ogre's insides with his needle sword, forcing the creature to spit him out and flee, leaving behind a magical hammer. The girl was so grateful to Issun-bōshi that she used the hammer to help him grow to six feet tall.

MAGICAL HAMMER
The *uchide no kozuchi* is a magical mallet (a type of hammer) that can make wishes come true. This mallet appears in a number of Japanese folktales. Issun-bōshi used one to help him grow in size, find treasure, and conjure up food.

A PERILOUS VOYAGE
For tiny Issun-bōshi, the voyage to the capital was a dangerous one. He used a bowl as a boat, a chopstick as an oar, a cup as helmet, and a piece of straw as a sheath for his needle-sword.

KNOW YOUR HERO

Stories about Issun-bōshi come from Japanese folktales dating back to the Muromachi Period of the 14th–16th centuries.

Despite being only 2.5 cm (1 in) tall, no bigger than his father's thumb, Issun-bōshi was known for being brave and strong.

He is famous for fighting an ogre to rescue a girl – he then married her and became a wealthy samurai.

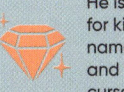

SIGURD
DARING DRAGONSLAYER

Valiant Sigurd was descended from Odin, king of the gods, but still fell prey to a terrible curse.

Both Norse and Germanic legends speak of Sigurd, the dragonslayer known for his legendary strength. His great courage made him chase the sparkling gold of the dragon Fáfnir. But Fáfnir's treasure carried a terrible curse, which would eventually cause Sigurd's death.

Sigurd used Gram, a sword specially forged for him, to attack the beast.

CURSED TREASURE

Fáfnir was a dwarf who stole his father Hreidmar's treasure and killed him. His endless greed turned him into a dragon. Fáfnir guarded his hoard of stolen treasure despite knowing that it had been cursed by a dwarf named Andvari – whoever owned it was destined to die. When the dragon met his end at the hands of Sigurd, the hero willingly took on the curse.

DYNAMIC DUOS

When pairs of siblings embark on adventures, their enduring bond helps them win even against terrible odds.

In legends from around the world, siblings prove themselves stronger together – dominating the battlefield, defeating enemies, and saving people. Some might play tricks on one another, but in the face of danger, they join forces. Here are some of the fiercest, boldest, and bravest sibling pairs.

Nakula   Sahadeva

VORVONG AND SORVONG
Khmer princes Vorvong and Sorvong were falsely accused of treason and exiled from their father's kingdom. The brothers went their own ways and set up their own kingdoms. But they eventually reunited, combining their armies and returning to their kingdom to take the throne back from their evil stepbrother (see p.101).

NAKULA AND SAHADEVA
Expert swordsmen, the twins Nakula and Sahadeva feature in the Hindu epic *Mahabharata*. They guarded their brother Arjuna's chariot and helped him capture King Drupada, who became an ally of the Pandavas in the Kurukshetra War (see pp.82–85). As well as being skilled fighters, Sahadeva was a wise astrologer, while Nakula was an able charioteer.

VÄINÄMÖINEN AND ILMARINEN
The Finnish epic *Kalevala* includes the adventures of Väinämöinen and Ilmarinen. While they were not brothers by blood, their fight against the witch-queen Louhi (see pp.124–125) brought them together, forging a strong bond of brotherhood.

CASTOR AND POLLUX
The ancient Greek twins Castor and Pollux were skilled horsemen who did everything together, such as hunting a monstrous boar and joining the Argonauts (see p.120). Even death couldn't keep them apart. When Castor was killed, the god Zeus transformed them both into gods.

BALIN AND BALAN
In tales of Britain's King Arthur (see p.34), the brothers Balin and Balan were skilled knights in Arthur's army. Their lives ended in tragedy when they faced each other in a joust. Dressed in full armour, the brothers failed to recognize each other and fought to the death.

AMPHION AND ZETHUS
Twin sons of Zeus, Amphion and Zethus were abandoned as children on a mountain, but survived when a passing shepherd took care of them. Amphion became a musician, while Zethus grew up to be a hunter. The pair built and fortified the Greek city of Thebes.

HENGIST AND HORSA
The Germanic twins Hengist and Horsa together led the first Anglo-Saxon invasion of the British Isles in the 5th century CE. Horsa was killed in the conflict, but his brother survived and founded the kingdom of Kent in what is now the southeast of England.

The flag of Kent features a **white horse,** inspired by Horsa's own flag.

TWIN FIGHTERS
MONSTER KILLERS

When the world was plagued with a series of nightmarish monsters, the twins Nayénzgan and Tobadzîschíni came to the rescue.
Tales of the miraculous twins are shared among the Indigenous Diné people (also called Navajo) who live in the southwestern US. Their father was a god, the Sun Bearer. He armed his sons with mighty weapons, including lightning, sunbeams, and deadly rainbows, to help them rid the world of its monsters.

NATURAL WONDERS
People often link their cultural legends to natural features such as mountains, trees, rocks, and water. Called the "Navajo Twins" by locals, these stone pillars in Utah, US, were shaped by the wind over millions of years. The Diné named this pair after the hero twins.

FEARSOME BEAST
The twins battle a monster called Yé'iitsoh (The Giant) in this Diné illustration from a picture book. This giant ate so many people that they nearly went extinct. The heroes peppered the beast with lighting-fast arrows, killing it.

KNOW YOUR HERO

The hero twins feature in the folklore of the Diné people, who settled in southwest US around 1,000 years ago.

They were the sons of the god Sun Bearer. The twins were brave warriors, and role models for the Diné.

They are famous for destroying many monsters that bothered the people, especially the fearsome Yé'iitsoh.

MAMA HUACO
WARRIOR QUEEN

Fierce and formidable, Mama Huaco was a skilled warrior who led armies into battle.
Mama Huaco's weapon of choice was a bola – a cluster of stones tied together, which spun through the air once thrown. But she did more than terrify her enemies. She was an able ruler of Cusco, the Inca city she helped to set up. She also planted and harvested the first corn, which was an important crop for the Inca people.

Mama Huaco was the **daughter** of the Sun and the Moon.

KNOW YOUR HERO

Mama Huaco is known from the legends of South America's Inca civilization, founded in the 13th century CE.

This warrior governed the city of Cusco with her husband Manco Cápac.

She is known for her part in founding Cusco, the Inca capital.

SKILLED TEACHER
Mama Huaco wears a traditional handwoven shawl called a *lliclla* in this painting from South America. She played an important role in teaching the Inca women how to weave thread into cloth.

Many Greek warriors fought with light spears known as javelins.

ACHILLES' HEEL

Achilles was born to the goddess Thetis and King Peleus. His mother tried to make him immortal by dipping him into the magical waters of the River Styx. Because she held him by one heel, this undipped part became his weak point.

ACHILLES
TERROR OF TROY

Unstoppable Achilles was bold, brave, and known throughout Greece for his exceptional fighting skills. He was a major character in the stories of the Trojan War in Homer's *Iliad*. Achilles was born mortal, so his mother held him by his heel as she dipped him in magical waters, making the rest of his body invulnerable. Achilles grew up to become the greatest Greek fighter of the Trojan War. Driven to a frenzy when the Trojan prince Hector killed Achilles' friend Patroclus, Achilles killed Hector. In the battle that followed, Hector's brother Paris fired an arrow that found its mark in Achilles' unprotected heel, injuring him fatally.

AVENGING PATROCLUS

When Achilles' closest companion Patroclus was killed in battle by the Trojan Hector, Achilles flew into a rage. He fought fiercely to avenge his friend, killing Hector in single combat before the gates of Troy.

HECTOR
TROJAN CHAMPION

The noble prince of Troy was the greatest Trojan warrior and the biggest obstacle for the Greeks during their siege of Troy.

Hector was the son of the Trojan king Priam. A champion fighter, he led the Trojan army in the conflict and inspired the people of Troy to defend their city against the attackers. He was not just a great warrior, but also a man of good character, who valued peace and justice. Although Hector was the single-most skilled warrior in the entire Trojan army, he died at the hands of Achilles, who was more than a match for him.

KNOW YOUR HERO

 Hector is a leading character in the tale of the Trojan War, which features in Homer's epic poem, the *Iliad*.

 Prince Hector was the heir to the city of Troy, and a skilled warrior who fought valiantly to defend it from the Greeks.

 An exceptional warrior, Hector was also level-headed and wise. He was a loving son, husband, and father.

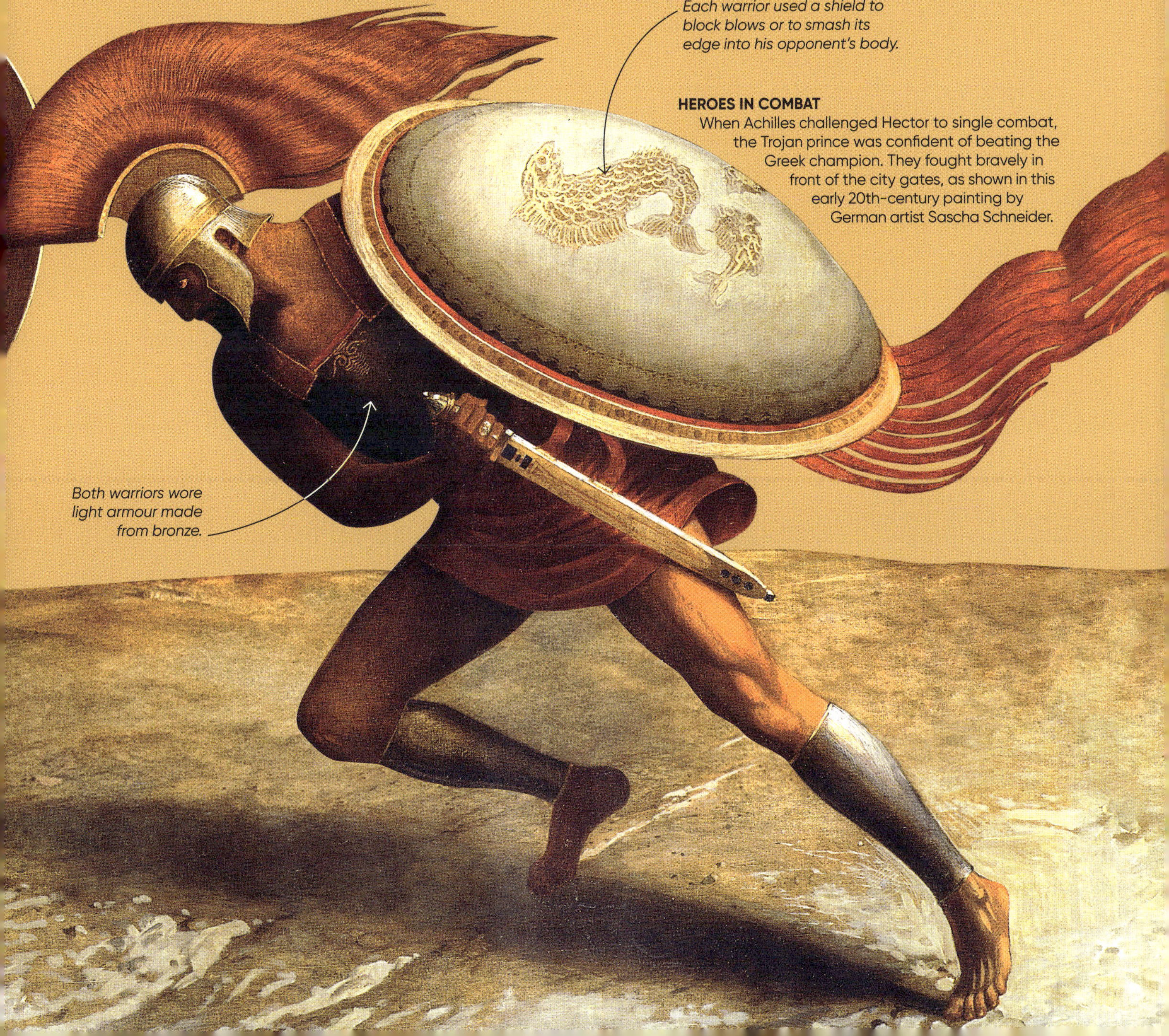

Each warrior used a shield to block blows or to smash its edge into his opponent's body.

HEROES IN COMBAT

When Achilles challenged Hector to single combat, the Trojan prince was confident of beating the Greek champion. They fought bravely in front of the city gates, as shown in this early 20th-century painting by German artist Sascha Schneider.

Both warriors wore light armour made from bronze.

THE TROJAN WAR

Centuries ago, Prince Paris of the city of Troy ran away with a Greek queen called Helen, triggering a great war. The Greeks besieged Troy for 10 years, but they struggled to breach its walls. Eventually, they tricked their way in, by making it appear they had given up and left a "gift" for their enemies. This was a colossal wooden horse, which the Trojans pulled into their city as a war trophy. Unknown to them, it was full of Greek soldiers, who climbed out at night to open the city gates to the rest of the Greeks and destroy the city. Some of the many great warriors of the war are shown here.

The wooden horse was Odysseus's cunning idea.

PANDARUS
A skilled archer, the Trojan Pandarus wielded a bow he made from the bones of a type of deer called an ibex. He wounded Helen's husband Menelaus with an arrow, and fought a duel with the Greek hero Diomedes.

GLAUCUS
A prince from Lycia, Glaucus fought on the side of the Trojans. When he found himself crossing swords with Diomedes, he realized their grandfathers had been friends. He nobly stopped the fight and the pair exchanged armour on the battlefield.

Paris was famously good looking.

PARIS
Troy's prince Paris fell in love with Helen, the wife of Menelaus, the first time he saw her. His doomed passion for Helen started the Trojan War, but he was protected by Aphrodite, the Greek goddess of love.

NESTOR

Nestor, the king of the city of Pylos, was older than almost every other warrior in the conflict. He fought for the Greeks, offering sage advice.

AGAMEMNON

It was King Agamemnon, Menelaus's brother, who united the Greeks to fight Troy. He commanded 100 ships, and led the combined Greek forces. He sacrificed his daughter Iphigenia to the goddess Artemis to create good weather for sailing to war.

Mighty Ajax wielded an enormous spear.

AJAX THE GREAT

Colossally tall, Ajax was the second-most powerful warrior among the Greek troops – only Achilles was stronger. He is famous for rescuing the body of Achilles from the Trojans, so that it could be honoured with lavish funeral rites.

MENELAUS

Helen's husband Menelaus was the king of Sparta. An able warrior, he challenged Paris to one-on-one combat to put an end to the long-running Trojan War. Just as Menelaus was about to win, the goddess Aphrodite whisked Paris away to safety.

DIOMEDES

Mighty Diomedes fought with the support of Athena, goddess of war. He was one of the Greek warriors inside the wooden horse, and was such a ferocious fighter that he managed to wound both the god Ares and the goddess Aphrodite in battle.

ATALANTA
SWIFT-FOOTED HUNTER

In ancient Greece, athletic Atalanta was fleet of foot and skilled with a spear and bow.

When she was a baby, Atalanta's father left her to die in the woods, but she survived in the wild. She grew up strong, fast, and fearless, and was an expert hunter by the time she joined a band of heroes pursuing the Calydonian Boar. Atalanta was the first to draw blood, and was awarded the boar's skin as her prize.

THE CALYDONIAN BOAR
The goddess Artemis was angry with the king of Calydon because he had failed to make offerings to her. So she sent a ferocious beast called the Calydonian Boar to ravage his kingdom. The boar is hunted down in this ancient Greek cup from the 6th century BCE.

KNOW YOUR HERO

Atalanta appears in myths from ancient Greece from around 800 BCE.

She was a skilled hunter, archer, and athlete.

Atalanta was the first to strike the Calydonian Boar.

READY FOR THE KILL
Atalanta is fully armed for a lion hunt in this Roman mosaic from the 4th century CE. Her legendary hunting skills came in handy when going after many wild animals and supernatural creatures such as centaurs.

YENNENGA
FEARSOME FIGHTER

Princess Yennenga was as brilliant at winning wars as she was at challenging rules and authority.
King Nedegea ruled over a kingdom in West Africa. His daughter Yennenga became an able warrior at a young age – at only 14, she was helping her father fight off enemies. As the princess led his fighters to victories, she became known far and wide as a fearsome warrior. She became so important to him that he refused to let her marry. Fed up with her father's restrictions, she eventually ran away from home.

Yennenga is known as the **mother** of the Mossi people.

RIDING INTO BATTLE
A horse's back was a second home for Yennenga, who was skilled with a spear.

KNOW YOUR HERO

 Yennenga is known from the folktales of the Mossi people, who live mainly in Burkina Faso.

 She was an extraordinary horse rider, a brave warrior, and an able military leader.

 She is famous for fighting and winning wars for her kingdom.

YENNENGA'S LEGACY
The fiery princess is remembered as an independent thinker who was prepared to push back against authority. An important award in African cinema is named after her: the Étalon de Yennenga ("Stallion of Yennenga"). French-Senegalese film director Alain Gomis (centre) won the award in 2017.

CHARGING INTO BATTLE
As a teenager, Cú Chulainn rode into war to defend the ancient kingdom of Ulster in the north of Ireland. He single-handedly defeated the invading army of Queen Medb of Connacht in the west. This illustration from 1911 by US artist Joseph Christian Leyendecker shows the hero in the heat of battle.

CÚ CHULAINN
HOUND OF CULANN

Celtic champion Cú Chulainn was a superhero in ancient times, with the strength to overcome any opponent.

Born to Deichtine, a princess of Ulster, this hero was known as Sétanta before he changed his name to Cú Chulainn, which means "hound of Culann". Trained by the warrior woman Scáthach, Cú Chulainn became the greatest knight of the Red Branch, an elite order of the king's warriors. When he rode into battle, a terrifying frenzy transformed him into a monster – he shook all over, his body parts shifted under his skin, and a light blazed from his forehead.

KNOW YOUR HERO

Cú Chulainn was born in the Irish province of Ulster. His stories date back to the 1st century CE.

No ordinary hero, Cú Chulainn is the central character of the Ulster Cycle, a set of early Irish heroic legends.

Best known for his astonishing feats as a warrior, he was regarded as Ulster's ultimate defender.

HOUND OF CULANN
At birth, Cú Chulainn was named Sétanta. When the guard dog of a blacksmith named Culann attacked the hero, he killed it in self-defence. Seeing Culann's grief at losing his protector, Sétanta vowed to become the protector of the kingdom, taking on the name "Cú Chulainn", which means "hound of Culann".

When a raven perched on the dead hero's shoulders, his enemies realized he was no more.

HURLING
A stick-and-ball game called hurling has been played for thousands of years in Ireland. It is the country's national sport. Many of the country's hurling clubs are named after Sétanta or Cú Chulainn, who played the game and used his hurling stick as a weapon to kill the guard dog of Culann.

BRAVE TO THE END
At only 27 years old, Cú Chulainn was fatally wounded by his own spears. He tied himself to a rock so that he could continue to stand and look his enemies in the eye, a hero to his last breath.

UNCOMMON ORIGINS

Not every hero was born from human parents: some of them had very unusual beginnings.

Some heroes were the children of gods, spirits, animals, trees, or even the ground itself. An unconventional parentage could bring these heroes both advantages and disadvantages. They could have special skills and powers, such as strength, speed, magic, and the ability to fly. But it could also mean that a hero had to overcome greater difficulties.

Asclepius could **raise the dead.**

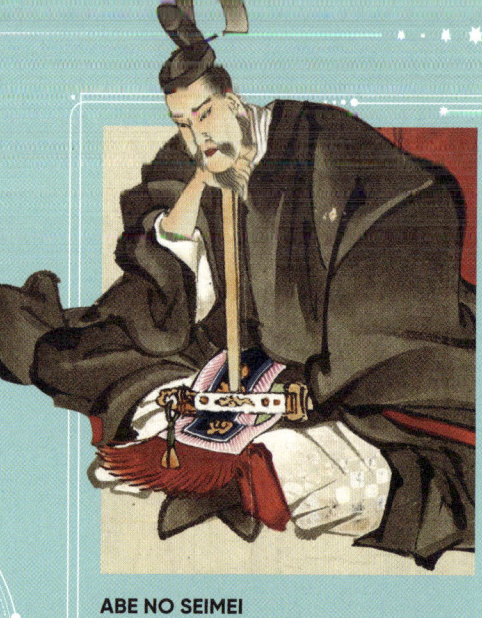

ABE NO SEIMEI
Born in the 10th century CE, Japanese court official and astrologer Abe no Seimei was said to be the son of a man and a kitsune (fox spirit). He lived to a great age and had incredible magical powers, which he used to heal people, foretell the future, and fight off evil spirits.

ASCLEPIUS
This ancient Greek hero was the son of a mortal woman and the god Apollo. Trained by his father and the centaur Chiron, Asclepius became a skilled doctor. Years after his death, he turned into the god of medicine. Sick people slept in his temples, hoping he would cure them in their dreams.

PYRRHA
The ancient Greek hero Pyrrha threw rocks that turned into women as they hit the ground. Her husband threw rocks that became men, and so the two of them created the whole of humanity. Pyrrha was the daughter of Pandora, a mortal, and Epimetheus, a Titan god.

IMHOTEP
Believed to be the son of the ancient Egyptian god Ptah, Imhotep was born an ordinary mortal. He served as the chief minister to Pharaoh Djoser but was also a scribe, architect, doctor, and high priest. Imhotep became such an important figure that he was made a demigod years after his death.

PENTHESILEA
The warrior-queen Penthesilea was the daughter of Ares, the ancient Greek god of war, and Otrera, a queen of the Amazons. She led an army of Amazons in the Trojan War but fell to the spear of the great hero Achilles (see p.58). As she died, she gazed at Achilles and the two fell in love.

Plaited rope symbolizes the Milky Way's trail of spirits in the sky.

ENMERKAR
Mighty Enmerkar was a king of the ancient Mesopotamian city of Uruk. He was the son of the Sun god, Utu. With help from his sister, the goddess Inanna, he used his vast knowledge and wisdom to defeat a wizard and capture the city of Aratta.

WIČAȞPI HIŊȞPÁYA
The son of a Lakota woman and a magical young man from the sky, Wičaȟpi Hiŋȟpáya ("Fallen Star") was born on Earth after his mother fell to her death through a hole in the clouds. He was raised by the Lakota people (who live in what is now North America) and grew up to be strong and clever. Before he returned to his father's people in the sky, he promised to watch over the Lakota in times of hardship.

Wičaȟpi Hiŋȟpáya rises to the sky in this enamel glass mosaic by Oglala Lakota artist Angela Babby.

MULAN
WARRIOR IN DISGUISE

As war raged in ancient China, Mulan took to the front line as the only female fighter among male warriors.
With her ageing father too weak for war, Mulan decided to take his place. In ancient China, only men were allowed to be soldiers, so Mulan disguised herself as a man. A master archer and expert horse rider, she brought her excellent fighting skills to the battlefield during years of conflict. After the war, when Mulan finally removed her armour, her fellow soldiers were shocked to see a woman among them!

STARTING EARLY
Many girls in ancient China were never taught how to fight, but Mulan's father trained her in the use of weapons from a young age. In this 19th-century pen and ink portrait, Mulan is seen stringing her bow in a garden, possibly to practise her archery skills.

A NATION AT WAR
Mulan's story is set in the Northern Wei Period (386–535 CE) in ancient China. This was a chaotic era in which different dynasties fought for supremacy, while also facing attacks from invaders and neighbouring tribes. Mulan joined the army to fight nomads from the north.

KNOW YOUR HERO

Mulan's tale comes from a Chinese song, the *Ballad of Mulan*, written between the 4th and 6th centuries CE.

Chinese writers depict Mulan as an exceptional soldier at a time when women were not allowed to serve in the army.

Mulan served in the imperial army for 12 years, and then went home.

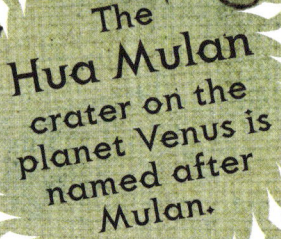

The Hua Mulan crater on the planet Venus is named after Mulan.

BRYNHILD
VALIANT VALKYRIE

The Norse god Odin's immortal female warriors, known as valkyries, appeared on battlefields to take the souls of the dead on their final journey to the afterlife. Brave Brynhild's physical strength was unrivalled among the valkyries. Brynhild's brute force surpassed every man but one – only the legendary hero Sigurd could match her power and prowess. They fell in love, but when Sigurd betrayed Brynhild by marrying the princess Gudrun, and tricked Brynhild into marrying Gudrun's brother Gunnar, she took revenge on him. All versions of this tale end in Sigurd's death.

HEROIC AFTERLIFE
The Old Norse word valkyrie means "a chooser of the slain". On Odin's orders, valkyries flew over battlefields, chose true heroes killed in battle, and carried them to Valhalla, the home of dead heroes. Brynhild is dressed in regal armour and ready for the battlefield in this 1898 painting by French painter Gaston Bussière.

FATEFUL ENCOUNTER
Brynhild was Odin's favourite, but when she disobeyed him, he took away her immortality and ordered her to marry a man as punishment. Then he put her to sleep inside a circle of fire. When Sigurd crossed the flames to awaken Brynhild, their ill-fated romance began.

KNOW YOUR HERO

 Brynhild features in different northern European legends that were first written down in the 13th century CE.

 In Norse tales, Brynhild is an immortal valkyrie and a warrior, but in Germanic legend she is a powerful warrior-queen.

 She is admired for her remarkable strength and courage, which combine to make her a fierce and fearless warrior.

KNOW YOUR HERO

Rostam was well known in Persia for centuries before the Persian poet Ferdowsi wrote the epic *Shahnameh* in the 10th century CE.

Born to a great general and a princess of Kabul (a city in Afghanistan), Rostam became Persia's greatest paladin (holy warrior) and folk hero.

The Persian prince enjoyed a long list of victories, especially the final defeat of Esfandiyār.

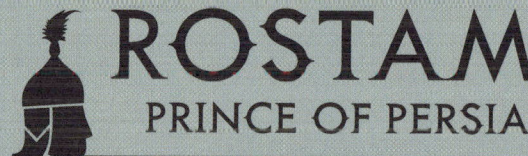

ROSTAM

PRINCE OF PERSIA

The greatest hero in Persian folklore was a warrior prince whose long life was truly epic.

As a young child, Rostam killed a rampaging elephant with one blow, and tamed a wild stallion called Rakhsh. Trained in warfare by his father, Rostam wore an extraordinary battle suit that protected him from fire, water, and weaponry, making him almost invincible. He rode his impressive stallion Rakhsh through his homeland and beyond on travels full of adventure. Fiercely loyal to the shah (king) of Persia (present-day Iran), he performed seven labours to save his monarch from demons, fought for his nation, and triumphed on the battlefield. His greatest victory of all was over Esfandiyār, another legendary warrior with an impenetrable suit of armour.

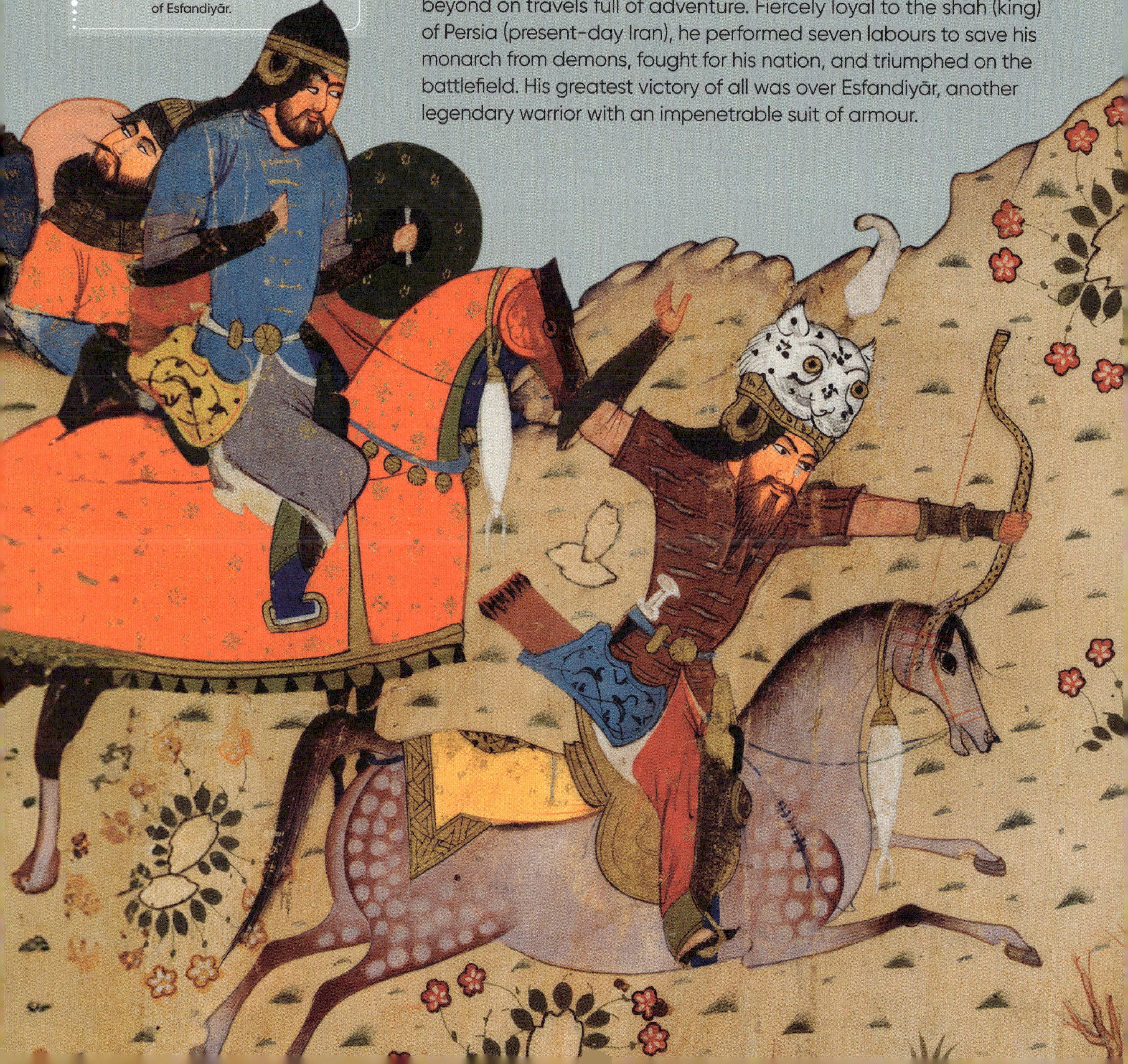

NATIONAL EPIC

The *Shahnameh* ("Book of Kings") is an epic poem written by the Persian poet Ferdowsi. More than 100,000 lines long, it describes the origins of the Persian Empire, and documents its history and culture. This scene from the *Shahnameh* depicts the court of the legendary Persian king Kay Khosrow.

A TRAGIC OUTCOME

Tragedy struck during a battle between the Persians and the neighbouring Turanians (a legendary people of Central Asia). Rostam killed a Turanian warrior, only to discover that this was his own son Sohrab. Rostam was devastated, as shown in this painting from the *Shahnameh*.

ARROW ATTACK

The prophet Zoroaster gave Esfandiyār a magical protective armour, so he could be killed only if he was shot in the eyes by a double-headed arrow. When Rostam found out, Esfandiyār's fate was sealed. The hero (leading the charge on the left) blinds Esfandiyār (in front on the right) with the special arrow in this 16th-century Persian painting.

Rostam and Rakhsh lived for **many** centuries.

THE ADVENTURES OF ROSTAM

When Shah Kay Kāvus's failed expedition led to his capture by the divs (demons) of Mazandaran, there was only one man who could save him. Prince Rostam's loyalty was put to the test as never before during the long journey to rescue his king. Together with his trusty steed Rakhsh, Rostam endured seven trials – a series of life-threatening ordeals that challenged his heroic strength and courage to the utmost.

Rostam slept through the lion's attack on his horse.

1 HUNGRY LION
At the start of the journey, a lion stalked Rakhsh. It pounced, sinking its claws into Rakhsh, hoping to make a meal out of the horse and its rider. But Rakhsh bit back and stamped on his aggressor. Rostam woke up to see his wounded horse and a dead lion.

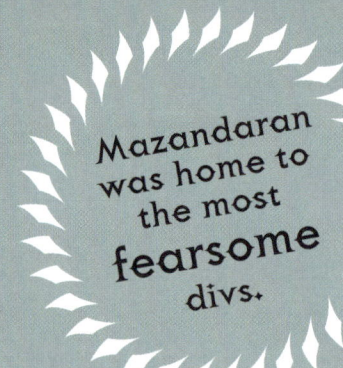

Mazandaran was home to the most **fearsome** divs.

2 A QUEST FOR WATER
Rostam and Rakhsh travelled to a scorching desert where they grew weak with thirst. The desperate hero turned to his god, and his faith was rewarded. Rostam received divine assistance in the form of a passing sheep that led him to a spring of cool water.

3 DEADLY DRAGON
One dark night, at the edge of a remote forest, an enormous dragon suddenly emerged. Rakhsh neighed loudly to warn his sleeping master – Rostam woke with a start and slayed the dragon on the spot.

4 DEMON IN DISGUISE
In an idyllic woodland with sparkling streams, Rostam encountered an enchanting sorceress. When he asked her to reveal her true identity, she turned into a dreadful demon. The hero wasted no time in killing the creature.

The sorceress was caught by Rostam with a noose around her neck.

5 CAVE OF DEMONS
Rostam came across a cave where he fought and defeated a band of demons single-handedly. He captured their champion, named Olad Div, and ordered him to be Rostam's guide for the rest of his journey.

6 RESCUED RULER
The epic journey ended when Rostam reached the city of Mazandaran and found Shah Kay Kāvus tied to a tree and blinded by the demons. Rostam killed Arzhang Div, the demon chief of Mazandaran, and set Kay Kāvus free.

Rostam dealt the fatal blow with his sword.

7 BATTLE TO THE END
Rostam's final test was a battle with Div-e-Sepid, the white demon of Mazandaran. The fighting was fierce, but Rostam prevailed. He used the blood from the demon's heart to restore the king's sight.

LANCELOT
NOBLE KNIGHT

Many classic British stories feature King Arthur's Knights of the Round Table, and Lancelot stood out as the bravest. Best known for his victorious battles and successful quests, this charming and chivalrous knight was just as effective at defeating dragons as rescuing royals. He was devoted to King Arthur's wife, Queen Guinevere, and played a major role in saving her from the clutches of the villain Mordred.

A VILLAIN'S LIES
Mordred, the king's treacherous nephew, plotted to steal the throne from Arthur and take Guinevere as his wife. He spread lies about an improper relationship between the queen and Lancelot. In this 1911 illustration by English artist Walter Crane, Lancelot fights off knights loyal to Mordred outside Guinevere's chamber.

DRAGON SLAYER
Killing a dragon was a heroic feat and a badge of honour achieved by only the bravest. This illustration from 1910 by English artist Arthur Rackham shows Lancelot's exceptional sword skills as he slays a dangerous, fire-breathing dragon.

KNOW YOUR HERO

Lancelot first featured in medieval European stories and poems from the 12th century.

Born in France, he is one of the most famous knights of the Round Table in Arthurian legends.

Renowned for his loyalty and bravery, Lancelot rescued Queen Guinevere when she was abducted, and killed a deadly dragon.

FIONN MAC CUMHAILL
DEFENDER OF IRELAND

This heroic hunter-warrior hailing from Ireland was blessed with brawn and brains in equal measure.

Fionn was raised by two warrior women who shared their skills with the young boy. After catching and tasting a magic fish called the Salmon of Knowledge, he gained all the wisdom of the world. He went on to lead a band of fierce young warriors known as the Fianna, and became a legendary champion of the Irish people, defending their country against all enemies.

DEFEATING AILLÉN
Fionn's greatest opponent was a fire-breathing monster named Aillén, whose bewitching music sent victims into a deep sleep before they were killed. Armed with his magical spear, Fionn stayed awake to plunge it through Aillén's heart and end the terror once and for all.

KNOW YOUR HERO

 Fionn Mac Cumhaill featured in the Fenian Cycle, a series of stories set in 3rd-century Ireland.

 A superb warrior and leader, Fionn was said to have a magic thumb that gave him great wisdom.

 Fionn is best known for leading a warrior band, the Fianna, and protecting his land from evil monsters.

Illustration of Fionn and Aillén by Irish painter Beatrice Elvery, made in 1914

CAÍLTE MAC RÓNÁIN

By far the fastest of the Fianna was Caílte, who fought using his special sword Cruadh-Chosgarach, meaning "the Hard Destroying One". When the king of Ireland captured Fionn, he demanded that Caílte bring him all the wild animals of Ireland to secure his release. Quick-footed Caílte completed this challenging task in a single day.

Fionn's spear, called the Birgha, had magical powers.

FIONN MAC CUMHAILL

The leader of the Fianna was blessed with all the world's wisdom after eating the Salmon of Knowledge (see p.75). He slayed deadly monsters, including a fire-breathing being from the underworld.

GOLL MAC MORNA

The invincible one-eyed warrior Goll was the strongest of the Fianna. He commanded the battlefield, disposing of enemies with ease. He had killed Fionn's father to become the leader of the group until Fionn proved himself a worthy replacement.

DIARMUID UA DUIBHNE
Brave Diarmuid single-handledly saved the Fianna by slaying more than 3,000 rivals during one attack. He used his spear to deadly effect.

THE FIANNA

The leafy forests of the Emerald Isle provided the perfect hideaway for a brave band of young Irish heroes, called the Fianna.
As guardians of Ireland, the Fianna roamed the land, confronting danger and battling enemies in a series of action-packed adventures. These Celtic heroes lived in the wild and hunted for survival. Only the elite could join them, warriors who had proven themselves to be fearless fighters Their stories were brought to life in the Fenian Cycle, a collection of stories set in ancient Ireland during the 3rd century CE. Some of the well-known members of the Fianna are depicted here.

OISÍN
Son of Fionn, Oisín shared his father's brains and brawn, but is best remembered for being a celebrated poet. He was the narrator of the Fenian Cycle and famously went to live in Tír na nÓg (Land of Youth) for 300 years.

ARASH
MASTER OF THE BOW

Skilful Arash was the best archer that ancient Persia had ever seen.
Arash could fire an arrow farther and faster than any other warrior in the army, and served his king with great loyalty. Persia (modern-day Iran) had been at war with its neighbour Turan for many years, but eventually the two sides agreed to end the fighting. The new boundary between the countries would be drawn based on how far Arash could shoot an arrow.

Arash's **voice** is said to guide people who get lost in Iran's mountains.

Arash's bow has magical powers in some versions of his story.

Brave Arash's tir (arrow) gave its name to Iran's Tirgan festival.

Bronze statue of Arash in Tehran, Iran's capital

FINAL SHOT
Arash climbed Mount Damavand in order to take his shot. He poured his whole life force into his arrow, sacrificing himself so that the arrow could fly for days to make his country as vast as possible. The moment he drew the bow is captured in this statue.

KNOW YOUR HERO

Arash is known from the legends of ancient Persia. He may have been born in the city of Ray.

He was a famous warrior, and particularly skilful with a bow and arrow.

Arash ended a 60-year war. On Iran's New Year's Eve, people look up at Mount Damavand in his honour.

Aphrodite

Aeneas

AENEAS
BRAVE PATHFINDER

Most men would be daunted if they saw their city crumble around them, but not Aeneas.
After Troy fell to the Greeks, the Trojan fighter Aeneas embarked on a long quest to find a new home. He travelled west to Sicily, and then on to Carthage in Africa, where he fell in love with the city's queen, Dido. Finally, he sailed to the River Tiber in Italy, bringing his people to a place that would one day become Rome.

WAR IN LATIUM
When Aeneas arrived in Italy, not everyone was happy to see him. Fighting broke out in the region of Latium, near the River Tiber. This statue shows Aeneas being given armour for battle by his mother, the goddess Aphrodite.

VISITING THE UNDERWORLD
Aeneas had a vision where his father Anchises urged him to visit the underworld to foresee his future. At the end of a perilous journey to the realm of the dead, Aeneas saw a vision of his descendants – including Romulus, the founder of Rome and a mighty empire.

Aeneas founded the city of Lavinium, near present-day Rome.

KNOW YOUR HERO

Aeneas is the central hero of the *Aeneid*, an epic poem written by the Roman poet Virgil in 30–19 BCE.

He was a famous warrior, and a member of Troy's royal family. His mother was Aphrodite, the goddess of love.

Like the Greek hero Odysseus, Aeneas is famous for his wanderings after the Trojan War.

KNOW YOUR HERO

Kintarō is a Japanese folk hero whose tales date back to Japan's Heian Period (794–1185 CE).

He was known for his superhuman strength – legend has it that his father was the ferocious thunder god Raijin.

As a child, Kintarō wrestled giant animals and killed monsters. He grew up to be a great samurai.

Kintarō's ono (axe) deals a deadly blow to the shrieking eagle.

FEATHERED FOE

Kintarō came face to face with countless wild creatures in his remote mountain home. In this 19th-century woodblock print, Japanese artist Kitagawa Tsukimaro captures the battle between Kintarō and a great eagle. As usual, his phenomenal strength meant there was only one winner.

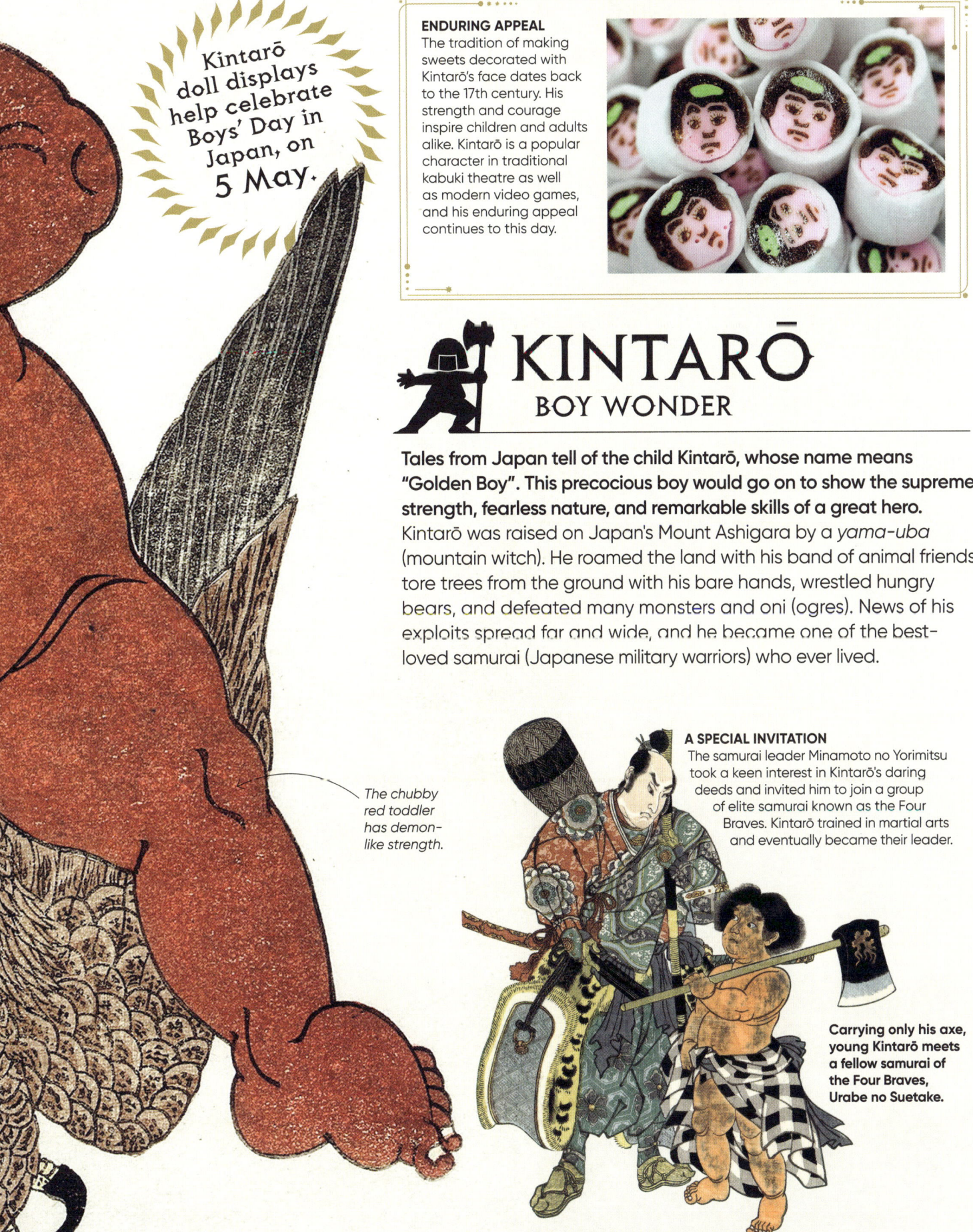

Kintarō doll displays help celebrate Boys' Day in Japan, on **5 May.**

ENDURING APPEAL
The tradition of making sweets decorated with Kintarō's face dates back to the 17th century. His strength and courage inspire children and adults alike. Kintarō is a popular character in traditional kabuki theatre as well as modern video games, and his enduring appeal continues to this day.

KINTARŌ
BOY WONDER

Tales from Japan tell of the child Kintarō, whose name means "Golden Boy". This precocious boy would go on to show the supreme strength, fearless nature, and remarkable skills of a great hero.
Kintarō was raised on Japan's Mount Ashigara by a *yama-uba* (mountain witch). He roamed the land with his band of animal friends, tore trees from the ground with his bare hands, wrestled hungry bears, and defeated many monsters and oni (ogres). News of his exploits spread far and wide, and he became one of the best-loved samurai (Japanese military warriors) who ever lived.

The chubby red toddler has demon-like strength.

A SPECIAL INVITATION
The samurai leader Minamoto no Yorimitsu took a keen interest in Kintarō's daring deeds and invited him to join a group of elite samurai known as the Four Braves. Kintarō trained in martial arts and eventually became their leader.

Carrying only his axe, young Kintarō meets a fellow samurai of the Four Braves, Urabe no Suetake.

ARJUNA
ACE ARCHER

KNOW YOUR HERO

 Arjuna is one of the main characters of the Hindu epic *Mahabharata*, which was written between the 3rd century BCE and 4th century CE.

 He was a Pandava prince from ancient India's Kuru kingdom (in what is now northern India).

 As one of the most skilled warriors in the Kurukshetra War, he played a major role in ensuring the victory of the Pandavas over the Kauravas.

One of the five royal brothers called the Pandavas in Hindu legend, Arjuna the archer features in many tales of valour from India. Arjuna showed his knack for archery at a young age, leaving his teachers awestruck at his skill. He was very loyal to his family and allies. During the Kurukshetra War between the Pandava princes and their cousins, the Kauravas, he slayed countless enemy warriors and commanders, peppering them with lightning-fast arrows before they had a chance to realize what hit them.

ARJUNA VS KARNA

The Kurukshetra War played out for 18 days on a battlefield called Kurukshetra. Arjuna single-handedly took on entire battalions of soldiers and killed many commanders, but his greatest foe was the Kaurava warrior Karna. Their face-off is depicted in this painting from northern India, made around 1820.

ARJUNA DANCES

A traditional dance from southern India is Mayilpeeli Thookkam ("The dance of Arjuna"). Arjuna performed it as a tribute to the goddess Kali for supporting him in the war. Today, this dance – featuring elaborate costumes – can be seen in temples as a ritual offering to the goddess.

Arjuna

Krishna, an avatar of the God Vishnu, drove Arjuna's chariot in the war.

KARNA
FEROCIOUS FIGHTER

A fearsome Hindu warrior known for his unrivalled fighting skills, Karna was invincible on the battlefield until fate intervened and brought his tale to a tragic end.

Abandoned at birth and set adrift on a river, the son of the Sun god Surya was found and raised by a charioteer and his wife. Karna grew up with the Kaurava and Pandava princes and trained to be a warrior. His fateful battle against his rival Arjuna has been recounted in countless tales set in ancient India.

A TEACHER'S CURSE
Most gurus (teachers) refused to teach Karna because he was the son of a common charioteer. So he went to the warrior sage Parashurama (left) and lied about his humble birth to become his student. But when the sage discovered Karna's lie, he cursed him so that Karna would forget all he had learned when he needed it the most on the battlefield.

KNOW YOUR HERO

Karna's story is told in the *Karna Parva*, the eighth of the 18 books that make up the epic *Mahabharata*.

This child of the Sun god Surya and Queen Kunti of the Kuru kingdom grew up to be a mighty warrior.

As a Kaurava commander in the Kurukshetra War, Karna was responsible for killing many of the Pandavas' warriors.

RISE AND FALL
Karna's extraordinary skills and loyalty to the Kaurava leader Duryodhana helped him rise up the ranks quickly. He commanded his own battalion during the Kurukshetra War. But on day 17 of the war, Karna forgot how to use his weapons because of Parashurama's curse, and was killed by Arjuna's arrow.

The elephant was a symbol of the Kaurava capital city Hastinapur ("elephant city").

Shalya, Karna's charioteer

Karna

THE WARRIORS OF KURUKSHETRA

The battlefield of Kurukshetra was the site of the epic conflict between rival cousins, the Pandavas and the Kauravas, for the throne of the Kuru Dynasty. Both sides of the family battled daily from sunrise to sunset in a war that turned many of the warriors into legendary heroes. Their feats were immortalized in the ancient Hindu epic, the *Mahabharata*.

DHRISHTADYUMNA

Legend goes that Dhrishtadyumna and his sister Draupadi were born from a holy fire lit by their father Drupada. Dhrishtadyumna entered the world as a grown man, battle-ready with armour and weapons. This warrior trained under Dronacharya, rising to the position of commander-in-chief of the Pandava army.

Abhimanyu rode into battle in his chariot.

ABHIMANYU

Arjuna's son Abhimanyu surprised the Kauravas by slipping into their impenetrable *chakravyuha* – a circular military formation made up of layers of soldiers. But this brave Pandava warrior became trapped inside – aged just 16, he fought hard before dying at the hands of seven Kaurava warriors.

BHIMA

The five Pandava princes were Yudhishtira, Bhima, Arjuna, Nakula, and Sahadeva. Arjuna's older brother Bhima was known as the strongest of the five. When they were children, the Kaurava leader Duryodhana tried to kill Bhima with a poisoned cake and dumped him in a river. There, Bhima met the Nagas (half-human, half-serpent beings), who cured him with their venom and fed him a potion that gave him the strength of 10,000 elephants.

GHATOTKACHA

The son of Bhima and a rakshasi (female monster) named Hidimbi, Ghatotkacha was a hybrid warrior. His superhuman strength and superb skills with weaponry helped him wreak havoc on the Kaurava army.

DRONACHARYA

A gifted archer, Dronacharya taught archery and warfare to the Pandava and Kaurava princes. During the Kurukshetra war, he fought on the side of the Kauravas. As long as he held a weapon, he was impossible to defeat, so the Pandavas used trickery to kill him. They lied that his son had been killed in battle. Grief-stricken Dronacharya laid down his weapons, and the Pandavas beheaded him.

BHISHMA

The great warrior Bhishma was the youngest son of the goddess Ganga and King Shantanu (the great-grandfather of the Pandavas and Kauravas). He became commander-in-chief of the Kaurava army during the war. Bhishma killed many soldiers in the Pandava army before he was stopped by Shikhandi (see p.99). Arjuna was able to shoot him down with arrows.

The bow was one of many weapons that Bhishma mastered with devastating effect.

DURYODHANA

The eldest Kaurava brother was an exceptional warrior. His ability with a gada (metal mace) was unmatched, allowing him to kill many opponents at once with one great swing. He was killed in battle by Bhima.

LĀČPLĒSIS
NATIONAL HERO

Abandoned at birth, Lāčplēsis was suckled by a wild bear.

Larger than life in Latvian legend, Lāčplēsis was a bear-battling, giant-duelling warrior chosen by the gods to protect Latvia.

When the Estonian giant Kalapuisis went on a rampage in Latvia, only Lāčplēsis was able bring him to his knees. Despite countless encounters with evil, he survived and fought Christian crusaders who threatened to conquer Latvia and replace its beliefs with their own. Today, Lāčplēsis is a national hero who stands for courage and strength.

FIGHT TO THE DEATH

Lāčplēsis once fought a warrior called the Black Knight. This illustration shows the pair in combat at a castle tournament. Legend goes that they will continue fighting to the death, and if Lāčplēsis ever wins, Latvia will truly find freedom.

KNOW YOUR HERO

Inspired by local folklore, Lāčplēsis's story comes from an epic published by Latvian poet Andrejs Pumpurs in 1888.

He is a Latvian hero who protected his country and his people during the crusades of the 12th–13th centuries.

Famous for his strength, Lāčplēsis is best known for slaying a bear and fighting Christian crusaders.

SLAYING THE BEAR

Lāčplēsis famously killed a wild bear to protect the lord who had adopted him as a baby. From then on, he was known as the "bear slayer". Unveiled in 1935 in the Latvian capital of Riga, this granite statue by Latvian sculptor Kārlis Zāle celebrates courage and freedom.

The story of Ilya Muromets dates back to 12th–13th century Russia. He was first mentioned in the 18th century in Russian folktales called *bylini*.

Ilya Muromets is one of the best known heroic knights from Russian folklore.

His many trials and tribulations included killing Nightingale the Robber and preventing numerous Tatar invasions.

CHANCE ENCOUNTER

Ilya Muromets became friends with the giant Svyatogor and they journeyed together to the Holy Mountains. Muromets encounters the giant in this 20th-century watercolour by Russian illustrator Ivan Bilibin.

ILYA MUROMETS
BOLD BOGATYR

From humble beginnings, Russian peasant Ilya Muromets made a meteoric rise to superhuman status.

Muromets spent the first 30 years of his life sitting on a stove, until some passing pilgrims helped him learn how to use his legs. The gift of a spectacular magical horse allowed him to leave home and ride off to the court of Saint Vladimir I of Kiev (in modern-day Ukraine). He became the chief *bogatyr*, or heroic knight, and famously killed Nightingale the Robber – a part-human, part-bird monster that had terrorized travellers for years.

When he died, Ilya Muromets turned to **stone.**

SUPER SAMURAI

The samurai were Japan's warrior class in the 12th–19th centuries. They served the samurai lords, or *daimyos*, who in turn answered to the ruling shogun. Samurai wore full body armour during battle to protect themselves.

Samurai body armour from the 12th century

INTO BATTLE

Tomoe Gozen tackles an enemy samurai with her bare hands while galloping into battle on her trusty steed in this 1750 woodblock print. Her excellent fighting skills and prowess with weaponry meant she disposed of rivals in seconds, taking out multiple enemies at a time.

KNOW YOUR HERO

Tomoe Gozen is remembered in the epic war poem *Heike Monogatari* ("The Tale of the Heike").

She is Japan's most famous *onna-musha* (female warrior). She lived in the Heian Period (794–1185).

Her unwavering courage and fighting skills in combat saw countless opponents fall on the battlefield.

TOMOE GOZEN
SWASHBUCKLING SOLDIER

Just her name struck fear into enemy hearts as this legendary fighter was said to be worth a thousand warriors on Japan's battlefields.

Tomoe Gozen was an *onna-musha* (female warrior) who led male warriors into battle. She commanded 300 samurai (elite warriors) and could defeat any demon or god that crossed her path. Her knowledge of martial arts and skills as an archer and swordswoman were invaluable during the 12th century, when Japan's warring clans fought for supremacy. Tomoe remained loyal to her samurai lord even after he faced defeat in the conflict.

Tomoe once guarded a bridge by herself against **dozens** of invaders.

THE SHOGUN
Japanese military leaders known as shoguns became powerful in the late 12th century. A young warrior called Minamoto Yoritomo defeated the rival Taira clan and became the first all-powerful shogun of Japan. He set up the Kamakura Shogunate (Japan's first military government).

TRIỆU THỊ TRINH
RAGING REBEL

Triệu Thị Trinh wielded a sword in each hand.

Known as Lady Triệu, this Vietnamese hero inspired her nation.
In the 3rd century CE, Vietnam was ruled by China. As a young girl, Lady Triệu was enraged by how poorly her people were treated. By the age of 19, this rebel had set up an army base training thousands of warriors. She won more than 30 battles before being defeated by Chinese forces.

Triệu Thị Trinh was said to have a voice as clear as a temple bell.

LEADING THE REBELLION
Triệu Thị Trinh spearheaded the Vietnamese rebellion, leading her troops in battle after battle against the Chinese army. In this painting, Vietnamese artist Xuân Lam shows her in combat mode, wearing a yellow tunic and riding her war elephant.

KNOW YOUR HERO

Triệu Thị Trinh is known from the legends of Vietnam and Chinese chronicles from c.980 CE.

She was a fierce warrior, 3 m (10 ft) tall, and led armies into battle.

A national holiday honours her brave resistance against China.

THÁNH GIÓNG
COLOSSAL COMBATANT

Mighty Thánh Gióng took on an entire army single-handedly to save Vietnam and restore peace.

As a small child, Thánh Gióng didn't talk or stand. When he was three, King Hùng VI sent messengers to his village looking for a hero to defend Vietnam against a Chinese invasion. Thánh Gióng surprised everyone by stepping forward. From then on, he began to eat a lot and rapidly grew 3 m (10 ft) tall. He defeated his enemies all by himself, on the back of his fire-breathing iron horse.

BAMBOO BATTLE
When Thánh Gióng's sword snapped in the middle of battle, he uprooted a bamboo plant to beat his enemy. The fire from his horse turned the bamboo yellow, with speckled burn marks.

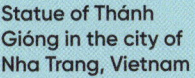

Statue of Thánh Gióng in the city of Nha Trang, Vietnam

GIFTS FROM A KING
King Hùng VI gave Thánh Gióng a series of gifts to help him in battle. There were colossal weapons, an iron helmet, and iron armour. Most spectacular of all was a fire-breathing iron horse, which Thánh Gióng is shown riding in this Vietnamese statue.

KNOW YOUR HERO

Thánh Gióng features in legends and tales from Vietnam, dating back to the 14th century.

He was an immortal defender of Vietnam, famous for his skills as a warrior.

Thánh Gióng is a national hero who fought off invaders and flew away never to be seen again.

{ HANG TUAH
LOYAL PROTECTOR

Malay hero Hang Tuah was a legendary fighter who devoted his life to serving the sultan of Malacca.

In the kingdom of Malacca in the Malay Peninsula, a young warrior caught the eye of Sultan Mansur Shah and became his most loyal admiral, ambassador, and protector. Under the sultan's orders, Hang Tuah defeated the famous Indonesian soldier Taming Sari in a duel to the death. When false rumours led to Tuah's exile, his closest friend Hang Jebat sought revenge by attacking the sultan – Hang Tuah had no option but to save his master by killing his friend.

ROYAL SHIELD
Hang Tuah protected the sultan from his enemies, guarding him on visits to other nations. He is shown in this stone relief armed with a powerful dagger.

Hilt of keris dagger

A hermit taught **martial arts** to Hang Tuah and his four friends.

KNOW YOUR HERO

 | |

Hang Tuah stars in the 17th-century book *Hikayat Hang Tuah* ("The story of Hang Tuah").

He is the model hero in Malay tradition, combining bravery and loyalty in equal measure.

Malay folk honour him for risking his life and sacrificing friendships to serve the sultan.

The famous Taming Sari keris is printed on this Malaysian postage stamp from 2006.

SPOILS OF WAR
Hang Tuah wielded a traditional Javanese dagger called a *keris*. It had belonged to the Indonesian warrior Taming Sari, but it was awarded to Tuah after he broke the dagger and won their duel. The magical weapon was so powerful that it could fight on its own.

Malaysia 2006   30 sen

Keris Taming Sari

MU GUIYING
GALLANT GENERAL

Brave warrior Mu Guiying led many armies to victory on the battlefield, protecting her land against invading forces.

Mu Guiying grew up in China during the Northern Song Dynasty (960–1127 CE). The daughter of a bandit, she was well trained in many martial arts. When the Song army faced powerful enemies and needed new leaders, Mu stepped up as a general and led many successful campaigns. Her most impressive victory was when she was only 19 and smashed the Liao army's Heavenly Gate military formation.

Mu Guiying wears the feathers of a military commander.

TAKING COMMAND
Mu Guiying rides a horse on this porcelain dish from China's Kangxi Period (1672–1722). The legendary commander was able to rally the troops of the Northern Song army with determination and clever strategy.

KNOW YOUR HERO

Mu Guiying appears in *Yang Jiajiang* ("The Generals of the Yang Family"), a collection of Chinese tales set in the Song Dynasty (960–1279).

This warrior from the Northern Song Dynasty is among the most successful female warriors in Chinese history.

Mu is most famous for standing up against the invasion of her land by the neighbouring Liao.

GANDIVA

The legendary bow known as Gandiva was created by Brahma, one of the three supreme Gods in Hinduism. Brahma made it to punish the wicked, and over the ages, it was wielded by several gods and a string of human heroes. The Pandava prince Arjuna (see p.82) used it in the Kurukshetra War, as written in the epic, the *Mahabharata*.

HERACLES' CLUB

The ancient Greek hero Heracles was incredibly strong, and wielded a giant wooden club carved out of a whole olive tree. He bludgeoned many monsters into submission with his club, including the two-headed hound Orthrus (see p.51).

The enormous bow was nearly impossible to break.

GÁE BOLGA

The legendary spear called the Gáe Bolga was created from the bone of a sea monster. The warrior woman Scáthach gave it to the Celtic hero Cú Chulainn (see p.64), who brandished it in battle (above). When thrown, the deadly weapon would hit its human target and expand into thirty barbs inside the body, ensuring certain death.

The Gandiva was powerful enough to fight 100,000 enemies at once.

TOOLS OF WAR

A hero's legend may not be complete without a mighty weapon or two to help them vanquish their enemies.

From clubs, axes, and bows to swords and spears, legendary heroes had many options when it came to picking their weapon of choice. While some weapons were created in a magical forge, or were gifts from gods, most reached their legendary status because of the incredible skill it took for a hero to wield them.

TELL'S CROSSBOW
Swiss hero William Tell (see p.155) used his crossbow to kickstart a rebellion and inspire his people to fight for their independence from Austrian rule. From deftly shooting an apple off his son's head to assassinating the tyrannical overlord Albrecht Gessler, Tell's crossbow never missed its mark.

GUAN YU'S GUANDAO
Chinese military general Guan Yu wielded the guandao – a heavy spear with a wide blade. He used this weapon to devastating effect on the battlefield, winning many wars. He was later immortalized as the god of war.

Excalibur was sheathed in a special scabbard.

BHIMA'S GADA
A gada is a type of mace or a heavy weapon with a round head and a spiked top. In the *Mahabharata*, the Pandava prince Bhima (see p.84), a strong man blessed with the power of 10,000 elephants, used his gada to crush his enemies.

EXCALIBUR
After his sword was shattered in a duel, King Arthur (see pp.34–35) went searching for a new weapon. One day, a mysterious figure known as the Lady of the Lake emerged from the watery depths of a magical lake to hand Arthur the legendary sword Excalibur. Its scabbard had the magical property of protecting its owner from wounds.

KUSANAGI–NO–TSURUGI
Originally used by the Shinto storm god Susano'o, this magical sword was passed down for generations until it was picked up by Japan's Yamato Takeru (see p.114). The hero discovered he could bend the wind with the sword, and used it to kill his enemies in a burning field by fanning the flames towards them.

DIHYA
BATTLE QUEEN

When the expanding Islamic empire arrived in North Africa in the 7th century CE, the Imazighen resistance was led by a brave woman: Dihya. Dihya was a princess who became a warrior-queen, with incredible military and leadership skills and the unusual gift of being able to see the future and predict an enemy's tactics. She united the nomadic tribes of the Imazighen (also known as Berbers) and led their armies against the Muslim invaders. She is still a symbol of revolution for Algerian people today.

The invading soldiers gave Dihya the name "Al-Kahina".

Imazighen spears had a wooden shaft tipped with an iron blade.

DEFIANT LEADER
Armed with a spear and the resolve to defend her kingdom, Dihya led her forces into battle against the invading armies. She had many victories, but was killed at the Battle of Tabarka.

KNOW YOUR HERO

 Dihya's legend was recorded by the Muslim historian Ibn Khaldun in the 14th century.

 Like her freedom-fighter father King Aksel, this warrior queen championed the Imazighen people.

 She is famous for leading her people against Muslim invaders.

KABUKI
In 1898, Japanese artist Toyohara Kunichika pictured a kabuki actor in this woodblock print. Japanese kabuki plays mix together acting and dance, with the actors wearing elaborate costumes and making stylized movements. Kabuki is still popular in Japan today and features a wide range of themes, including the hero Hangaku Gozen's bravery.

LEADING THE TROOPS

Hangaku's family was involved in struggles against a number of powerful Japanese clans. She led the troops defending her family's castle, raining arrows down against the invaders. Artist Taiso Yoshitoshi created this 1885 woodblock print showing her fully armed and mounted on horseback.

HANGAKU GOZEN
FIERY LEADER

One of the very few warrior women in 12th-century Japan, Hangaku Gozen's military training made her a deadly opponent. Gozen became a skilled warrior, famous for her bravery, discipline, and incredible talent with a bow and arrow. When her family became involved in military conflict against the Kamakura shogunate, Hangaku joined the fight. She led 3,000 warriors in battle against a much larger army of 10,000 soldiers. Although she was wounded by an enemy arrow and captured, her tale turned into legend.

KNOW YOUR HERO
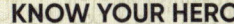

 Hangaku Gozen appears in a 13th-century chronicle of Japanese history.

 She was a great warrior and military leader, particularly skilled with a bow and arrow.

 She made it into the history books for being one of the few *onna-musha* (fierce warrior women).

KNOW YOUR HERO

 The first mention of Aliguyon is in traditional Filipino *hudhud* songs, which existed around the 7th century CE.

 He was a famous Filipino folk hero who would face any opponent to ensure peace for his village, Hannanga.

 Aliguyon is remembered as a warrior who could do battle for years without tiring.

Aliguyon was so **fast** he could catch any weapon thrown at him.

FAMOUS FIGHT
Aliguyon's biggest battle was against Pumbakhayon, the son of his father's enemy. The pair fought an epic duel for three years, but finally both warriors called a truce, became firm friends, and united their villages. Their conflict is pictured on this book cover by Filipino artist Ferdinand Doctolero.

ALIGUYON
BRAVE BATTLER

Fearless Aliguyon waged war against enemy invaders to protect his beloved mountain home in the Philippine islands. Legend goes Aliguyon could do battle without even resting or eating. His father was the chief of the Ifugao tribe, and taught him how to make and use a spear and shield. Determined to defend his village and his people, he fought in many battles. Some of these raged for years, yet Aliguyon never backed down and remained a proud peacekeeper for the village. The islanders pay homage to their local hero by bursting into songs about him during annual celebrations.

HUDHUD
The Ifugao people of the Philippines have shared storytelling songs – known as *hudhud* – for centuries. These songs often describe ancestral heroes and religious practices. Aliguyon remains a popular subject in *hudhud*, especially at harvest time or during the rice-sowing season.

THE THREE PRINCESSES

Bhishma was offended by the king of Kashi, so he abducted the king's daughters Amba, Ambika, and Ambalika (below). Amba wanted to marry another king, but when he rejected her, she turned to Bhishma instead. Bhishma's refusal to marry her drove Amba to kill herself. She vowed to take revenge on Bhishma in her next life.

BATTLING BHISHMA

Bhishma recognized Shikhandi as the former Princess Amba, so he refused to fight him – fighting a woman went against a noble warrior's creed. Seeing his chance, Shikhandi led the charge on Bhishma, and Arjuna shot him down with a volley of arrows. Bhishma was killed in this battle, and Shikhandi's revenge was complete.

SHIKHANDI
STEADFAST AVENGER

A remarkable tale of revenge and reincarnation in the Hindu epic *Mahabharata* introduced the brave warrior Shikhandi.

The hero Shikhandi had a serious axe to grind. In a previous life, Shikhandi was Princess Amba of Kashi. When she was wronged by Bhishma of the Kuru kingdom, she swore vengeance in her next life. Reborn as Shikhandini, she later transformed into a man named Shikhandi, who made it his mission to kill Bhishma. In the Kurukshetra War, he finally succeeded with the help of Prince Arjuna.

KNOW YOUR HERO

Shikhandi features in the Hindu epic poem *Mahabharata*, written between the 3rd century BCE and 4th century CE.

He was originally a princess called Amba, who was wronged by Bhishma and swore to take revenge in another life.

Shikhandi is famous for triumphing over his enemy Prince Bhishma.

Arjuna

Bhishma

Shikhandi

EKLAVYA
STAR PUPIL

Raised in the forest, Eklavya dreamed of becoming a master archer in a thrilling tale from Hindu mythology.

Eklavya was eager to learn archery from Dronacharya, a skilled archer who taught only the princes of the Kuru kingdom. So Eklavya secretly taught himself by watching the teacher's methods. He soon became more skilled with a bow and arrow than Dronacharya or the princes, a feat that led to his downfall.

KNOW YOUR HERO

Eklavya's tale comes from the Hindu epic poem *Mahabharata*, written down in ancient India around 2,000 years ago.

He was a talented archer, known for his skill with a bow and arrow.

Eklavya is famous for cutting off his thumb as a sign of devotion to his teacher.

Prince Arjuna, Dronacharya's royal pupil

Dronacharya

PAYING THE PRICE

When Dronacharya found out that Eklavya had become skilled at archery by following his techniques, he charged a fee, asking Eklavya for the thumb of his right hand. Eklavya so revered his teacher that he cut off his thumb in an instant – despite knowing it meant he could never again draw his bowstring and shoot an arrow.

Eklavya cuts off his thumb in this 20th-century illustration by Indian artist Shri Vitthal Das Rathore.

Vorvong
decapitates his
evil stepbrother.

VORVONG
PRINCE IN EXILE

Betrayed and exiled, Prince Vorvong undertook a remarkable journey to return home and clear his name.

In ancient Khmer folklore, Vorvong and his younger brother Sorvong were sent away from their kingdom on false charges of treason. The brothers became separated, and wandered alone for 10 years. Overcoming every obstacle, including a flesh-eating giant, Vorvong finally reunited with his brother to go into battle together and reclaim their kingdom.

FINAL BATTLE
Mounted on a war elephant in this illustration from a 19th-century book of Khmer folktales, Prince Vorvong kills his wicked stepbrother with a single stroke of his long-handled sword. Triumphant, Vorvong and Sorvong could at last return to the palace and tell their father the truth.

FALSELY ACCUSED
The person responsible for Vorvong's woes was his stepmother, who wanted her own son to inherit the throne. She made up such wicked stories about Vorvong and his brother that the king ordered them to be executed. The executioners lead them away in the picture above, but the princes escaped unharmed and went into exile.

KNOW YOUR HERO

Vorvong is known from ancient Khmer folktales, which come from the land that is now Cambodia.

The Khmer prince used his wits and wisdom to become the ruler of three kingdoms.

Vorvong famously defeated his evil stepbrother and won back his father's trust.

DARING ADVENTURERS

Intrepid heroes set off on the trip of a lifetime to follow their dreams, rescue true loves, or save their people. They travelled far and wide, crossing land, sea, and sky on epic journeys. Their boldness and bravery was only strengthened by the many dangerous encounters and obstacles they had to overcome along the way.

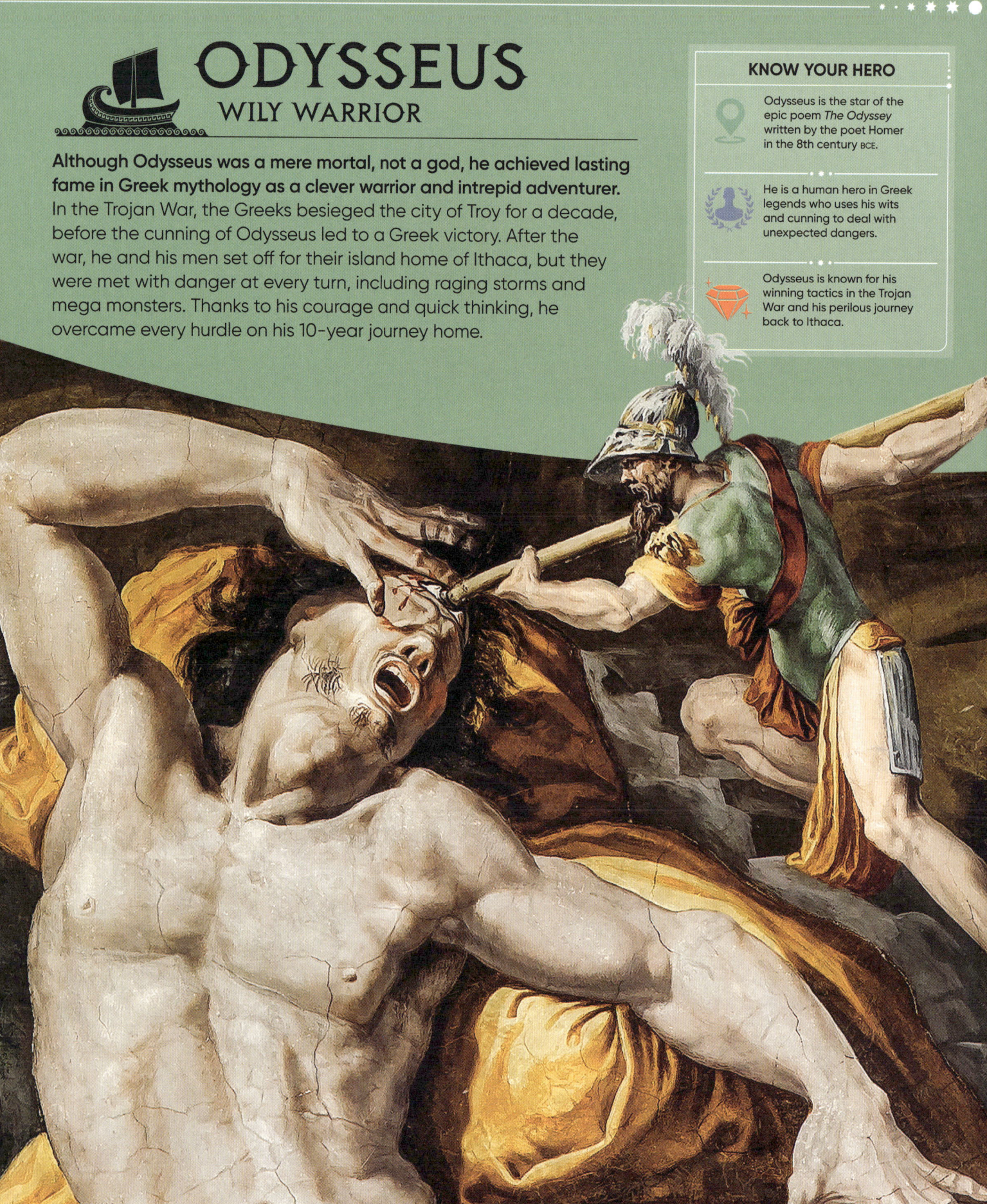

ODYSSEUS
WILY WARRIOR

Although Odysseus was a mere mortal, not a god, he achieved lasting fame in Greek mythology as a clever warrior and intrepid adventurer. In the Trojan War, the Greeks besieged the city of Troy for a decade, before the cunning of Odysseus led to a Greek victory. After the war, he and his men set off for their island home of Ithaca, but they were met with danger at every turn, including raging storms and mega monsters. Thanks to his courage and quick thinking, he overcame every hurdle on his 10-year journey home.

KNOW YOUR HERO

Odysseus is the star of the epic poem *The Odyssey* written by the poet Homer in the 8th century BCE.

He is a human hero in Greek legends who uses his wits and cunning to deal with unexpected dangers.

Odysseus is known for his winning tactics in the Trojan War and his perilous journey back to Ithaca.

PERIL AT SEA
Half-woman, half-bird, the sirens sang enchanting songs that lured passing sailors to jump overboard and drown. Odysseus wanted to hear their song and survive. So he had his crew plug their ears with wax and tie him to the ship's mast – as seen in this mosaic from 260 CE.

WAIT AND WEAVE
Odysseus was apart from his wife Penelope for two decades, but her love never faltered. Many men asked to marry Penelope, thinking Odysseus was dead. To avoid their attention, she asked her suitors to wait until she finished weaving a tapestry – a task she would never complete because she wove in the day and undid it at night.

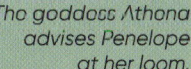

The goddess Athena advises Penelope at her loom.

BLINDING POLYPHEMUS
Odysseus was once stranded on an island that was home to Polyphemus, who was a flesh-eating Cyclops – a one-eyed giant. This 16th-century fresco (wall painting) in Italy shows Odysseus driving a stake through the monster's only eye and blinding him so that he and his crew could escape.

THE ORDEALS OF ODYSSEUS

After a decade spent fighting in the Trojan War, the Greek hero Odysseus longed to return to his beloved island home of Ithaca. But his tumultuous voyage over land and sea saw him battle natural disasters, terrifying monsters, and dangerous magic that made him question whether he would ever reach his final destination.

1 STOLEN SUPPLIES
Odysseus and his army of at least 600 men arrived in the city of Ismaros, home of the Cicone people. They needed to stock up with food and water for the journey ahead, but Odysseus's men ransacked the city in search of loot. When the Cicones fought back, killing half a dozen men from each ship, the survivors had to flee.

2 FORBIDDEN FRUIT
After storms drove Odysseus off course for nine days, the wind carried him to the land of the Lotus Eaters, a group of people who survived by eating the lotus fruit. They shared the sweet-tasting fruit with three of Odysseus's men, who suddenly became drowsy. Forgetting any thoughts of home, all they wanted was to stay and eat more fruit. Odysseus dragged them back to the ships, and quickly set sail.

Odysseus rammed a stake through the giant's only eye.

3 CONFRONTING A CYCLOPS
The next stop was an island belonging to a flesh-eating cyclops (a one-eyed giant) called Polyphemus. He trapped Odysseus and his crew in a cave, but Odysseus saved the day by blinding Polyphemus, so they could run back to their ships unseen. The giant's father, the sea god Poseidon, vowed to later take revenge.

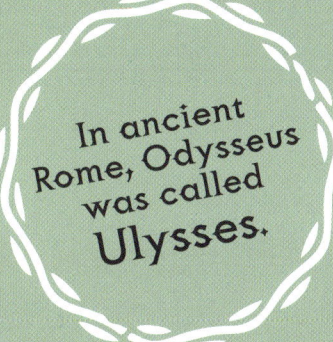

In ancient Rome, Odysseus was called **Ulysses.**

4 BLOWN BY THE WIND

On the island of Aeolia, Odysseus met the wind god Aeolus who gave him a leather bag. Inside were all the winds he needed to sail home. But back on board, his crew couldn't resist opening the bag in the hope that it contained riches. The winds were released, blowing the ships straight back to Aeolia. By now, the wind god had had enough and refused to help them on their way.

Most ships were damaged by the rock-throwing giants.

5 LAND OF GIANTS

Odysseus ran into more trouble on the rocky island city of Telepylos, the land of the cannibalistic Laestrygonian giants. The hungry giants ran down to the shore and started destroying the ships to stop the men leaving. Odysseus set sail as quickly as possible – his ship and crew were the only ones to survive.

The sailors were transformed into pigs as a punishment for taking advantage of Circe's island.

6 CIRCE'S ISLAND

Odysseus continued sailing to the island of Aeaea, home to the immortal witch-goddess Circe. She used her magic to transform some of the crew into pigs. The messenger god Hermes had already given Odysseus a herb called moly to avoid her spell. Persuaded by Odysseus, Circe turned pigs back into his sailors again.

7 FINDING HIS FATE
During the journey Odysseus descended into the underworld, the realm of the dead. There he met the spirit of an old, blind prophet named Tiresias who warned Odysseus that eating the cattle of the Sun god Helios would be punished by death. He predicted a safe return to Ithaca for Odysseus, but not for any of his crew.

Cliff-dwelling Scylla swallowed sailors whole between her sharklike jaws.

8 SCYLLA AND CHARYBDIS
Navigating the narrow Strait of Messina, Odysseus faced a tough choice between sailing past the six-headed, sailor-munching monster Scylla or the dreaded whirlpool Charybdis. Fearing he could lose his ship, he chose Scylla as the lesser of the two evils. This insatiable monster gobbled up six of his crew.

The swirling waters of Charybdis dragged down any ships that happened to pass by.

9 CATTLE OF THE SUN
Remembering Tiresias' advice, Odysseus hoped to avoid Thrinacia, the island home to the cattle of the Sun god Helios. But his exhausted crew were now starving, and despite the warnings of Tiresias, they hunted down and tried to eat the sacred cattle on this island. When Helios told Zeus, the king of the gods, he punished the sailors by drowning them in a shipwreck. Odysseus was now the last man standing.

10 CALYPSO'S CAPTIVE
All alone, Odysseus washed up on the island of Ogygia. A nymph named Calypso appeared and soon developed an obsession with the brave hero. She kept him captive on her island for seven years although he longed for home. It was only on Zeus's order to release him that she finally let him build a raft and leave.

Calypso gave Odysseus food, water, and clothes for his journey home.

11 FRIENDLY WELCOME
After Poseidon destroyed his raft in a storm, Odysseus found himself on the island of Scheria, home of the Phaeacians and their king Alcinous. After listening to Odysseus's story of his intrepid adventures, the king gave him a ship as fast as a falcon for the final stretch of his voyage.

12 LOVE CONQUERS ALL
When Odysseus made it home to Ithaca, he donned a disguise and discovered his devoted wife Penelope surrounded by suitors. Penelope promised to marry any man who could string Odysseus's bow and shoot an arrow through a row of 12 axes, but she knew that only her husband could accomplish this feat. Odysseus completed the challenge, shot his rivals, and revealed his true identity. Reunited with his family, he reclaimed the throne of Ithaca – his arduous, ten-year journey was finally at an end.

KUPE
TRAILBLAZING EXPLORER

A fisherman and explorer named Kupe made his mark on Māori mythology by discovering the breathtaking islands of Aotearoa (also known as New Zealand).

When a terrifying giant octopus began eating his fishing bait, Kupe chased it from his Polynesian home of Hawaiki, ultimately reaching the place called Aotearoa by the Māori. It was one landmass until Kupe cut a channel through the middle to create the north and south islands. These became home for the Māori people.

KNOW YOUR HERO

 While Kupe has appeared in oral Māori stories for centuries, the first written records date from 1849.

 This legendary Māori explorer was a great chief of Hawaiki (present-day Tahiti).

 Kupe discovered Aotearoa (New Zealand) and killed a monstrous octopus terrorizing his people.

HOT PURSUIT
Heading east from Hawaiki, Kupe kept going until he hunted down the giant octopus Te-Wheke-a-Muturangi. Kupe finally killed the sea monster with the help of his friend Ngake, as shown in this illustration by Māori artist Cliff Whiting.

PAIKEA
WHALE RIDER

The Māori speak of a brave boy named Paikea who rode a whale across the dangerous waters of the Pacific Ocean.
As his father's favourite son, Paikea suffered at the hands of his jealous half-brother. When he survived an attempt on his life at sea, Paikea found himself adrift in a canoe. He chanted a magic spell to call on a whale and calm the turbulent waters. A whale answered his call and carried him all the way to Aotearoa, which became a safe new home for him.

TO THE RESCUE
The whale that saved Paikea was called *tohorā*, and is said to have been a southern right whale. These ocean giants migrate thousands of kilometres each year, calling to each other with songs, and leap playfully from the waves. Paikea surfs the waves on the back of his saviour in this illustration by Māori artist Cliff Whiting.

KNOW YOUR HERO

 The Māori story of Paikea has been shared for centuries across the Polynesian islands.

 This traditional Māori folk hero was a courageous boy with magical abilities.

 Paikea is known and loved for calling a whale to his aid and riding it across the ocean to Aotearoa.

PERCEVAL
GRAIL SEEKER

Pure of heart and noble of mind, Perceval was a hero in Arthurian legend who succeeded in his quest to find the Holy Grail, the ultimate prize for Christian knights. Until he was a teenager, Perceval lived a simple life in a Welsh forest with his mother. His life was transformed when his heroic deeds led King Arthur to make him a knight of the Round Table. Perceval did battle with dangerous opponents and, like the other knights, he set off on the quest for the Holy Grail. After years of searching, he finally found it.

The Fisher King welcomes Perceval to his palace.

The Grail

A MISSED OPPORTUNITY
The Fisher King was a guardian of the Holy Grail, a golden chalice with magical powers. While fishing, he met Perceval and invited him to a feast at his palace. Perceval spotted the Grail there, but did not ask any questions about it and vowed to return. Only three knights are said to have found the Grail – Perceval, Bors, and Galahad, son of Lancelot.

Perceval slayed the Red Knight with a single spear.

Perceval's childlike innocence made him worthy of finding the Grail.

KNOW YOUR HERO

French poet Chrétien de Troyes' 12th-century work *Perceval, the Story of the Grail* is one the earliest known tales about this famous knight.

Perceval is one of King Arthur's noblest knights of the Round Table.

He is best known for defeating the Red Knight and fulfilling the knightly quest to find the Holy Grail.

THE RED KNIGHT

Perceval battles the Red Knight in this mural from 1883–84 by German artist August Spiess. When this villain stole a cup from King Arthur, Perceval killed him as punishment. Then Perceval donned his opponent's armour and became known as the Red Knight himself.

NOBLE HERO

Time and time again, Perceval's deeds showed his heroic nature. In this 19th-century illustration, he helps a lion save its cub from a serpent. Lions represented bravery and honour in Arthurian legends, reflecting Perceval's traits.

HOLY GRAIL

Christian knights searched far and wide for the Holy Grail because they believed it had been used by Jesus Christ, which gave it miraculous powers. The dove in this illustration of the Grail is a symbol for the Holy Spirit.

YAMATO TAKERU
MASTER OF DISGUISE

Brilliance and bravery went hand in hand for Japanese hero Yamato Takeru.

Born Prince Ousu no Mikoto, son of the 12th emperor, this legendary warrior was considered godlike among mere mortals. He was hot-tempered and fiercely patriotic, defending himself and his nation by donning disguises, deceiving enemies, and challenging deities. Some people say that when Yamato became sick, he transformed into a white bird and took flight, never to be seen again.

CLEVER TACTICS
Disguised as a woman, the prince fooled and defeated the chief warrior of the Kumaso tribe in southern Japan. When his identity was revealed, Prince Ouso was given the more familiar name Yamato Takeru, meaning "The Brave of Yamato", a reference to his province.

Yamato's sword is also known as the "grass-cutting sword".

A LASTING LEGACY
Prince Yamato is revered as a deity at shrines across Japan. Every November, people celebrate Tori no Ichi ("Festival of the Rooster") at Yamato's shrines, praying for luck and plentiful harvests. Markets next to these shrines come alive with shops selling lucky charms called *kumade* (above) and other items symbolizing good fortune.

FIRE ESCAPE
When enemy tribesmen set light to a field where Yamato stood, he took decisive action. As the fire raged, he used his special sword to slice away the grass and create an escape route – as shown in this 19th-century Japanese woodblock print by Ogata Gekkō.

SINDBAD
SPIRITED SAILOR

In the search for fame and fortune, Sindbad the sailor embarked on seven adventure-filled voyages, discovering amazing creatures, people, and places along the way. Stories of courageous Sindbad were inspired by the voyages of Arabic and Persian merchants and sailors in the 8th and 9th centuries. Sindbad met giant people, birds, and snakes on his journeys, and even crossed paths with cannibals! His ships faced many perils at sea, but this quick-thinking hero always found a way out – often laden with treasure. After his adventures were over, Sindbad retired with his family and wealth in his hometown of Baghdad (in modern-day Iraq).

HITCHING A RIDE
Rocs were enormous, ferocious birds that fed their offspring elephants and rhinoceroses. Sindbad encountered rocs more than once during his travels and even hitched a ride on a roc's leg in his second voyage.

KNOW YOUR HERO

Sindbad features in *One Thousand and One Nights*, a collection of stories from Southwest Asia and North Africa.

A restless explorer, Sindbad went on a total of seven sea voyages across the Indian Ocean.

Sindbad is famous for his amazing adventures at sea and in the incredible lands he visited.

Sindbad was shipwrecked on six of his seven voyages.

Sindbad stands in shock and fear at the sight of the giant serpents.

NAVIGATING THE SEAS
Sailing was dangerous and shipwrecks were common in ancient times. In the 15th century, Arab sailors began using the astrolabe as a navigation tool. It had a map of the sky, which they used to measure the height of the Sun and stars above the horizon at different times of day. This helped them to work out how far east or west they were travelling.

THE VALLEY OF SNAKES
His second voyage took Sindbad through a valley filled with millions of diamonds, guarded by snakes that could swallow an elephant whole. With his pockets full of diamonds, Sindbad escaped by attaching himself to a large piece of meat and tricking a giant roc into carrying him away.

OUTWITTING A TRICKSTER
On his fifth voyage, Sindbad faced a villain called the Old Man of the Sea. He tricked people into carrying him on their shoulders to cross a stream and refused to let go until they died of exhaustion. Sindbad broke free by getting him drunk. In this 1913 illustration by French-British artist Edmund Dulac, Sindbad is shown carrying the Old Man.

THE SEVEN VOYAGES OF SINDBAD

Sindbad was the son of a wealthy merchant, but after he squandered his inheritance, he was determined to go to the sea to make his fortune afresh. Each of his seven voyages brought its own series of dangers and rewards. Each time, he came home wealthier than ever, but this restless explorer still yearned for more adventure before finally retiring to a life of peace.

1 WHALE ISLAND
On his first voyage, Sindbad landed with his crew on a remote island. When they started a fire to cook a meal, the island began to twitch, then plunged beneath the waves. It was, in fact, a whale, and it dived beneath the waves, hurling Sindbad into the sea. Miraculously, he survived.

2 SNAKE ESCAPE
Discovering a jewel-studded island sounds like a good way to get rich, unless you get stuck in a valley full of giant snakes. Sindbad made his dramatic escape by attaching himself to a piece of meat covered in diamonds, which was carried off by a roc (giant bird) to its nest. Soon, other diamond-hunters rescued him.

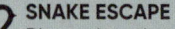

The large roc could grab an elephant easily in its talons.

3 DEATH BY GIANT
Hairy apes stole Sindbad's ship, leaving him and his crew stranded on yet another island. There, a giant began to eat the crew. Sindbad used hot iron rods to blind him and escape.

4 TOO THIN TO EAT
Sindbad came under threat from another set of cannibals on his fourth voyage. They drugged the crew, and began fattening them up. Sindbad refused to eat, and was allowed to go free because he looked too thin to be appetising.

5 ROAST ROC
Sindbad's crew found a giant roc egg and broke it open to roast the chick for dinner. Unfortunately for them, the parent birds soon appeared, and took revenge on the foolish sailors. Only Sindbad managed to escape alive.

6 TREASURE ISLAND
On his sixth voyage, Sindbad was shipwrecked on a mountainous island full of treasure. Eventually, he built a raft, piled it with riches, and floated down a river into the heart of a mountain and out to safety.

7 FLYING HIGH
On his final voyage, Sindbad came across a city where people could change themselves into birds. He rode one of these birds up to the heavens, but then he found out they were evil spirits. This was the last straw for Sindbad, and he decided to end his travels.

JASON
STEADFAST SEAFARER

Born a prince in the ancient Greek kingdom of Iolcos, brave Jason undertook a challenging quest to prove his royal birthright.

Young Jason was sent away to live on Mount Pelion after his uncle became king. Years later, he returned to his kingdom to reclaim the throne, which had been promised to him if he could retrieve the magical Golden Fleece. So Jason obtained a ship called the *Argo*, assembled a band of heroes known as the Argonauts, and set off on a perilous voyage to faraway Colchis in the east.

THE GOLDEN FLEECE

The legendary fleece from a winged, golden ram hung on a holy tree. Before he could reach it, Jason had to attach two monstrous oxen to a plough, fight a magical army, and then overcome a snake that guarded the fleece. The sorceress Medea gave him herbs to put the snake to sleep.

Medea

Jason

Jason was raised by **Chiron**, a famous centaur.

KNOW YOUR HERO

The tale of Jason and the Argonauts was told by Apollonius of Rhodes around the 3rd century BCE in his epic poem *Argonautica*.

This ancient Greek hero was the son of Aeson, king of Iolcos in Thessaly. He was a strong warrior and the leader of the Argonauts.

Jason is best known for his dangerous mission to retrieve the famous Golden Fleece.

ORPHEUS
MOURNFUL MINSTREL

The music that Orpheus played on his lyre was so beautiful that it could bewitch people, gods, and even stones. Long ago in ancient Greece, Orpheus fell in love with Eurydice, but their happiness was short-lived. The day after their wedding, tragedy struck – Eurydice was bitten by a poisonous snake and died. Consumed by grief, Orpheus set out for the underworld to rescue his beloved wife.

MAGICAL MUSIC
Orpheus's musical skills were superhuman. The lyre he played was a gift from Apollo, the god of music. The music he played held wild animals, trees, and even rocks spellbound.

KNOW YOUR HERO

This Greek myth has inspired poets and musicians from at least the 6th century BCE onwards.

Orpheus's skill in music was second to none, apart from the god Apollo himself.

He is famous for his attempt to rescue his wife from the underworld.

Orpheus

Eurydice, painted by Austrian artist Friedrich Heinrich Füger, c.1800

DON'T LOOK BACK
When Orpheus entered the underworld, Hades, god of the dead, was so moved by his singing that he agreed to let Eurydice leave, on one condition – Orpheus must not look back at her on the way out. Orpheus led the way, but he could not hear her footsteps. Worried, he glanced back at his wife, leaving her trapped in the underworld for ever.

SAVITRI
Princess Savitri married Satyavan, even though she knew he had only one year to live. When the Hindu god of death Yama took him, she travelled to the underworld to beg the god to spare Satyavan. Yama was moved by her love and devotion, and restored her husband to life.

OLLANTAY
Against all odds, an Inca tale of forbidden love between the fearless warrior Ollantay and Princess Kusi Qoyllur found a happy ending. Kusi's father, Emperor Pachacuti, rejected his daughter's lowly suitor, so Ollantay declared war. But he was captured after years of fighting, by the next Inca ruler, who pardoned him. The hero was now free to marry his love.

POPOCATÉPETL
The Aztec princess Iztaccíhuatl died of a broken heart after being told a lie that her warrior love Popocatépetl had died in battle. The hero was devastated by the news of her death, so he carried her up a mountain and never left her side. The gods transformed them into volcanoes to keep them together forever.

ROMANTIC HEROES

Many legends feature heroes who have proven beyond all doubt that love conquers all.
Faced with dangerous conflicts, tough challenges, epic journeys, and unexpected betrayals, many heroes risked their lives in the quest to win and protect their true loves. Time and again, they displayed the same traits of strength, courage, and resilience. They remind us that love can inspire us to face any challenge, no matter how difficult or frightening.

AMADÍS OF GAUL
The knight Amadís of Gaul fell in love with Princess Oriana, daughter of King Lisuarte of England. To prove himself worthy of Oriana's love, he took on wicked sorcerers, monstrous beasts, and aggressive invaders and eventually won her hand in marriage.

BRADAMANTE
Nothing could stop Bradamante's love for her fellow knight Ruggiero in the epic poems of the Holy Roman Empire. They had first met on the battlefield, but their different faiths kept them apart until Bradamante rescued her beloved when he was held captive in the castle of the sorcerer Atlante.

FARHAD
In Persian folklore, a sculptor named Farhad competed with King Khosrow for Princess Shirin's love. The king set Farhad the impossible task of carving a path through a mountain. Shirin visited Farhad to see his work, but her horse injured itself on the way back. Farhad then carried the princess and her horse home on his back. Sadly, Farhad died of grief when Khosrow sent him false news about her death.

DIARMUID
Daughter of the king of Ireland, Gráinne was destined to marry the old chief Fionn Mac Cumhaill (see p.75). But a chance meeting with the warrior Diarmuid changed her fate. The couple fell in love and ran away together. To save his beloved, Diarmuid fought off Fionn's men who came after them. The warrior met his death when he tried to hunt a wild boar fated to kill him.

SUNK IN THE SWAMP
A young magician
called Joukahainen came across
Väinämöinen on a narrow path
in a swamp, and a musical duel
followed. When Väinämöinen won,
he sank his opponent into the mud.
Väinämöinen's duel is captured in this
20th-century painting by Finnish
artist Joseph Alanen.

VÄINÄMÖINEN
MASTER MUSICIAN

Immortal Väinämöinen is the star of ancient folksongs – and of Finland's national epic, the *Kalevala*, which means "land of heroes".

Väinämöinen was a wise leader, warrior, healer, and bard – he could bend animals and people to his will with just a tune from his kantele. He once journeyed to a place called Pohjola, where the woman he wanted to marry set him a series of near-impossible tasks. These ranged from peeling a stone to splitting a hair with a blunt knife. Then the woman's mother, an evil bird-witch called Louhi, promised her daughter's hand in marriage to any man who could make a magical object called the Sampo. When the smith Ilmarinen forged the Sampo, Louhi sent him away and hid the object. Väinämöinen and Ilmarinen embarked on a perilous voyage with the hero Lemminkäinen to steal it back.

BARDS
Before TV, radio, and print, bards entertained people with songs and stories handed down from one generation to the next. Bards appear in many myths and legends – including those of the Celtic peoples, which feature the warrior-poet Oisín (above).

BATTLE FOR THE SAMPO
White-haired Väinämöinen and his band of heroes fought the winged witch in a ferocious sea battle to claim the Sampo, as seen in this painting by Finnish artist Akseli Gallen-Kallela. This magical object could produce salt, flour, and gold, but it was smashed to pieces during the fight.

Väinämöinen was born as an **old man** with a white beard.

Finnish people made kantele strings from horsehair.

MAGICAL KANTELE
Väinämöinen invented the kantele, a harp-like instrument, using the jawbone of a fish called the pike. His own kantele was magical, and charmed all those who heard its beautiful music.

KNOW YOUR HERO

Väinämöinen is the hero of the Finnish national epic, the *Kalevala*, published in the 19th century.

This Finnish folk hero is immortal, and has incredible musical skill and magical powers.

He is famous for journeying to the land of Pohjola and fighting the evil bird-witch Louhi.

BARI
SELFLESS SAVIOUR

Determined to save her parents, Princess Bari made a perilous quest to the underworld. Bari's father, the Korean king, had six daughters. He desired a son, so when he had a seventh daughter, he left her to die. But Bari was rescued by the gods. When the king and queen became sick with a deadly disease, selfless Bari journeyed to the underworld to find a cure and save them.

The resurrection flower grew only in the underworld.

KNOW YOUR HERO

Bari's story dates back 2,000 years to an ancient kingdom in what is now North Korea.

She was a princess who later became immortal, a shaman guiding the souls of the dead to the next world.

She is admired as a dutiful daughter for bravely going to the underworld to save her parents.

FLOWER OF LIFE
Bari was the only one of the seven princesses brave enough to make the journey to the underworld. A resurrection flower found there could save her ailing parents. By the time she got back, her parents had died – but the flower allowed her to bring them back to life.

Bari means "cast away" in Korean.

Princess Bari wears traditional royal attire in this 18th-century painting from Korea.

LEMMINKÄINEN
INTREPID TRAVELLER

Lemminkäinen was everything a Finnish hero should be: brave, strong, and prepared to go to the end of the world to get what he wanted. Lemminkäinen was set on marrying the daughter of the powerful witch-queen Louhi. Louhi was unhappy with the match and set three near-impossible tasks he had to complete first. Fulfilling these tasks took the hero on an incredible adventure, which included an arduous journey to Tuonela, the realm of the dead.

KNOW YOUR HERO

Lemminkäinen features in traditional Finnish songs and in the 19th-century epic poem *Kalevala*.

The young adventurer charmed women with his songs and undertook a daring quest to win his bride.

He is most famous for making a dangerous journey to the underworld.

A MOTHER'S LOVE
When Lemminkäinen's mother discovered that her son had been killed, chopped into pieces, and thrown into the River Tuoni, she was heartbroken. She went to the underworld to collect his remains and sewed them back together again – as seen in this 1897 painting by an unknown artist. Then she asked a bee to bring honey from the gods, which brought him back to life.

THE EVIL COWHERD
Lemminkäinen's final task was to kill the sacred swan that lived on the River Tuoni, which separated the world of the living from Tuonela. Sitting by the river was the cowherd Märkähattu who killed Lemminkäinen (right) and threw his body into the river. The fatal encounter is captured here by Finnish artist Joseph Alanen in this painting from 1919–1920.

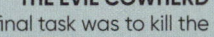
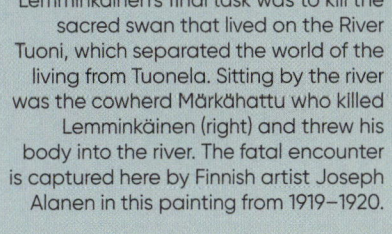

HUNAHPU & XBALANQUE
TWIN HEROES

The daring twins Hunahpu and Xbalanque made a death-defying journey through the realm of the dead to avenge their father's death.

The lords of Xibalba, the underworld, invited the twins to take part in a ball game rigged to ensure they would lose. The two heroes had to overcome a series of lethal challenges before they could even play. They dodged knives, built a fire in freezing temperatures, and fed bones to jaguars so as not to be eaten themselves. Ultimately, they used their cunning to trick the deities – defeating them for good and avenging their father.

DEITY OF MAIZE
The twins' father, Hun Hunahpu, was killed in the underworld by the lords of Xibalba. After Hunahpu and Xbalanque avenged his murder, he was reborn as the Maya deity of maize. He is linked to creation and regrowth in Maya culture.

KNOW YOUR HERO

Hunahpu and Xbalanque are key figures in the stories of the Maya, in central America.

The twins are the children of the hero Hun Hunahpu and Blood Moon, the daughter of an underworld deity.

They are famous for visiting the Maya underworld, and surviving their adventures there.

IN THE UNDERWORLD

Hunahpu and Xbalanque (above right) wait in the court of the underworld lord Its'amnaj (on the left) in this illustration from a Maya vase made in about the 7th century CE. The lords of the underworld challenged the twins to a ball game, secretly hoping to kill them using a ball that was really a skull with a hidden blade. When the brothers discovered the deceit, they objected to it, and were allowed to use their own ball. Their agility and skill helped them beat the deities at their own game.

PLAYING BALL

The game that the twins played in the underworld is one of the oldest sports ever recorded. This ball game from ancient Mesoamerica is known to have been played in Mexico more than 3,000 years ago. In it, players try to knock a rubber ball through stone hoops set on a wall.

Camazotz, a fearsome bat deity who drank blood, features on this Maya vase.

LORD OF XIBALBA

The Maya underworld is called Xibalba. Maya artists often represented it by showing the terrifying figure of the deity Camazotz. In the *Popol Vuh*, a sacred text of a group of the Maya peoples, Hunahpu and Xbalanque hid from Camazotz and narrowly escaped his clutches during their trials in Xibalba.

FINAL VICTORY

To finish off the lords of the underworld, the twins had to let themselves be killed in order to be reborn with magical powers. Then they tricked the deities into killing themselves with the promise of bringing them back, but instead, they left the lords for dead. After their mission was over, the twins rose into the sky – Hunahpu became the Sun and Xbalanque turned into the Moon.

FLYING TO HEAVEN
Etana nursed an eagle back to health, became friends with it, then rode it skywards towards the gods. After more than one attempt, they finally succeeded. Etana rides on the eagle's back (top right) in this seal from ancient Mesopotamia (modern-day Iraq) around 2250 BCE.

ETANA
SHEPHERD KING

Etana decided to ride an eagle to heaven to ask for a magical plant that would give him his greatest desire – a son and heir. After a great flood devastated the world, the gods created the city of Kish in what is now south-central Iraq, and chose the shepherd Etana as its ruler. He was a wise man who brought stability and prosperity to his kingdom, which thrived under him. But Etana was childless, and desperately desired a son to carry on his legacy. The Sun god Shamash guided him in his quest.

GREAT FLOODS
Around the world, ancient stories feature great floods like the one before Etana's reign. In the Babylonian *Epic of Gilgamesh*, the god Ea warns Utnapishtim about the flood and instructs him to build an ark (below) to save his family and each type of animal. In the Hebrew Bible, Yahweh (God) tells Noah to do the same, and in Hindu tales, a fish warns Manu, the first human.

KNOW YOUR HERO

Etana appears in the legends of Sumer, an ancient civilization in Mesopotamia (in present-day Iraq).

This great king is said to have ruled over the Sumerian kingdom of Kish for 1,560 years.

He is famous for flying to heaven on an eagle and was granted the magical "plant of birth".

LOYAL TO THE END
When Yudhishthira reached the gates of heaven, the gods were happy to let him in if he abandoned his canine companion. Yudhishthira valued the dog's loyalty and refused to do so. The gods praised him for his moral values, and let them both in.

YUDHISHTHIRA
FAITHFUL FRIEND

Wise Yudhishthira journeyed all the way to heaven, and insisted on taking his dog in with him.

Yudhishthira was a virtuous man who led the Kuru Dynasty after winning the Kurukshetra War. Thirty-six years later, he gave up his kingdom to seek heaven. He began his epic journey with his wife Draupadi, his Pandava brothers, and a dog, but his human companions perished on the way. When he reached the gates of heaven, the dog was denied entry, so Yudhishthira refused to enter heaven without his loyal follower.

KNOW YOUR HERO

 Yudhishthira features as a hero in the *Mahabharata*, a 2,000-year-old epic poem from Hindu mythology.

 This noble king was the eldest of the five Pandava brothers, and always sought truth and justice.

 Yudhishthira is known for journeying to the top of the Himalayas to reach the gates of heaven.

CHAMPIONS OF THE PEOPLE

Some heroes were dutiful protectors who risked their own lives to defend their communities or nations. Nothing stood in their way, as they took on invaders, monsters, tyrants, or natural disasters. They could also serve as messengers, bringing gifts from the gods to make the lives of their people better.

SNARING THE SUN
Māui saw that the Sun moved across the sky too quickly for people to finish their work during the day. So he threw anchored ropes into the sky to snare it and slow it down – as shown in this 21st-century block print made by artist Dietrich Varez in Hawai'i.

KNOW YOUR HERO

 Māui appears in the myths of the Polynesian islands in the Pacific Ocean. His stories have been told for over 1,000 years.

 This hero is part-human, part-god, and had a giant fish hook that gave him shapeshifting powers.

 He also used his intelligence, strength, and heart to improve the lives of the Polynesian people.

MĀUI
HEROIC HELPER

The legendary tales of this hero are told far and wide by islanders across the Pacific Ocean.

Abandoned as a baby, Māui was saved by the gods and granted special powers. He became a shapeshifter who could change into different animals. Māui was a trickster who made mischief, often annoying the gods, but he was also keen to help his people. Nothing was impossible for this Polynesian powerhouse – to improve the lives of his people, he lifted the sky over the islands, brought longer days of sunshine, and added fuel to make fire.

PLAYING WITH FIRE

To bring fire to the people, Māui tricked the fire goddess Mahuika into giving him each of her fiery fingernails until she was left with one. The furious goddess smashed her last nail on the ground, sparking an inferno. Māui escaped the flames by shapeshifting into a hawk as seen in this print by New Zealand artist E Mervyn Taylor. Before the fire was snuffed out, the goddess saved the dying sparks in some trees, which the people could use to make fire.

Māui hauled up Hawai'i from the seabed on his magical fishing hook.

MAKING ROOM

Legend has it that there was a time when the sky hung low over the land, making it difficult for plants to grow and for people to stand up. Māui solved the problem by raising the sky with his bare hands, in exchange for some water from a woman. Artist Dietrich Varez captures this incredible feat in this painting.

THE BIG SHRINK
At first, Glooscap made the animals very large – the beaver was gigantic in size and could build massive dams that stopped entire rivers. Later, he shrunk them down, making them smaller so they would be less dangerous for the humans.

Glooscap was said to be the first human, but far taller.

Box made of birch bark and porcupine quills

TEACHING SKILLS
The people learned all sorts of useful skills from Glooscap. He showed them how to use birch bark to make homes, canoes, and other everyday items, and how to build traps for fish, identify plants that were useful medicine, use fire, and make pottery. The tradition of using birch bark for craftwork has always been important in Mi'kmaq communities.

GLOOSCAP
GREAT CREATOR

The Indigenous Wabanaki peoples living in North America talk of mighty Glooscap, who had the form of a human but the powers of a god.

Glooscap appeared on Earth with his twin brother Malsum, when the world was all water. Soon he set to work shaping the empty world — he used his magical powers to create oceans and forests, as well as fairies and animals. He made humans by shooting his arrows into the trunks of birch trees. Glooscap became their protector, keeping them safe and teaching them useful things for survival. Malsum tried to spoil Glooscap's work, but Glooscap always prevailed.

When sleeping, Glooscap stretched across Nova Scotia.

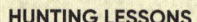

HUNTING LESSONS
Glooscap taught the people how to hunt animals for their meat and skins. He showed them how to make bows and arrows with sharp stone tips and how to scrape and clean animal hides so they could be used as clothing. Glooscap hunts a whale in this 19th-century illustration.

HIGH TIDES

The Bay of Fundy in Canada has the highest tides in the world. According to Mi'kmaq legend, Glooscap was responsible. He ordered a beaver to build a dam so he could take a bath. Angered by the water being held back, a whale struck the dam with its tail, resulting in high tides.

GUARDING HIS PEOPLE

The Mi'kmaq, Maliseet, Passamaquoddy, Penobscot, and Abenaki peoples form an Indigenous group known as the Wabanaki. Glooscap is an important figure in their folklore. This statue of him stands guard over a Glooscap Heritage Centre in Nova Scotia, Canada.

KNOW YOUR HERO

Glooscap is a founding father in the folklore of many Indigenous peoples living in what is now North America.

He is a cultural hero, known for his power over the natural world.

Glooscap is famous for being the first human, and for teaching people many useful skills.

Fibreglass was used to make this statue of Glooscap, which stands 12 m (40 ft) tall.

AMIRANI
SUPER HELPER

The demigod Amirani was born strong, and grew more powerful with every passing year.

Amirani stands out in tales from Georgia for his superhuman strength, impressive stamina, and super speed – all of which he put to good use in fighting ogres and dragons. As his powers grew, the gods felt threatened. When he tried to help humanity, the gods were enraged and they imprisoned him for all time in the Caucasus Mountains.

SLAYING THE OGRE
When brave Amirani came across a monstrous devi (ogre), he drew his sword and killed it, but three dragons sprung from its body. Amirani kept fighting, killing two of the dragons, but the third swallowed him up. That wasn't enough to stop the hero – he killed the beast from within and emerged unscathed.

KNOW YOUR HERO

 Amirani is the hero of a Georgian folk epic that has been told for centuries.

 The son of the goddess Dali and a hunter, Amirani was a fierce champion of his people.

 He is famous as a warrior with superhuman strength who fought off and defeated all sorts of monsters.

Amirani is celebrated in this Soviet postage stamp from 1989, when Georgia was part of the Soviet Union.

ETERNAL PUNISHMENT
Amirani was hailed as a hero (left), but when he shared the divine art of metalworking with humans, the gods became furious and punished him for challenging their supremacy. They locked him up inside a mountain, using magical chains they repaired every time he broke them.

АМИРАНИ илл. В. ОШ[ВАНИ]

10 к 1989 ПОЧТА СССР

МОСКВА

ENDLESS AMBITION
A great hunter and horseman, Oghuz would ride out to face monsters that threatened his people. Unsatisfied with being just the Khan of the Turks, he dreamed of reaching the four corners of the world in his quest to become the greatest Khan.

Oghuz Khagan hunts with a falcon in this 15th-century miniature painting.

Oghuz Khagan was guided by a **grey wolf** in many battles.

OGHUZ KHAGAN
UNSTOPPABLE TURK

The legendary Prince Oghuz Khagan went on to rule over the Turks.
Prince Oghuz learned to speak early and grew up quickly – in only a few weeks. He became a skilled warrior, who took it upon himself to rid his people of a terrifying dragon called Kiyant. Oghuz battled the beast, before chopping off its head. Stories about his bravery spread, turning into legend. Later, he defeated his father and become the Khan (ruler) of all Turks.

KNOW YOUR HERO

Oghuz Khagan is a central figure in Turkic mythology, with his legend shared across Central Asia and beyond.

The son of a Turkic ruler, Oghuz was a revered warrior, leader, and ancestor of the mighty Ottoman Dynasty.

He is known for uniting the Turkic peoples under his rule and becoming Khan of the Four Corners of the World.

SLAYING CORMORAN
Cormoran was a gruesome giant with an appetite for people and cattle. Jack set a trap by digging a pit for him to fall inside. This 19th-century engraving shows the moment Jack swung his pickaxe and Cormoran met his fate.

JACK
GIANT KILLER

There was no better giant killer in Cornish legend than the local farm boy Jack, who outwitted a string of colossal rivals.
Although the giants made him look small, Jack's sharp brain and unwavering courage ensured that he always came out on top. Killing Cormoran earned him the nickname "Jack the Giant Killer", but he also slayed others such as Blunderbore and the two-headed terror Thunderdell.

KNOW YOUR HERO

The earliest known version of Jack's story is *The History of Jack and the Giants* printed in 1711 in Newcastle, UK.

Young Jack became a folk hero by slaying giants to protect the people of Cornwall.

He killed so many giants that he was made a knight of the Round Table by King Arthur.

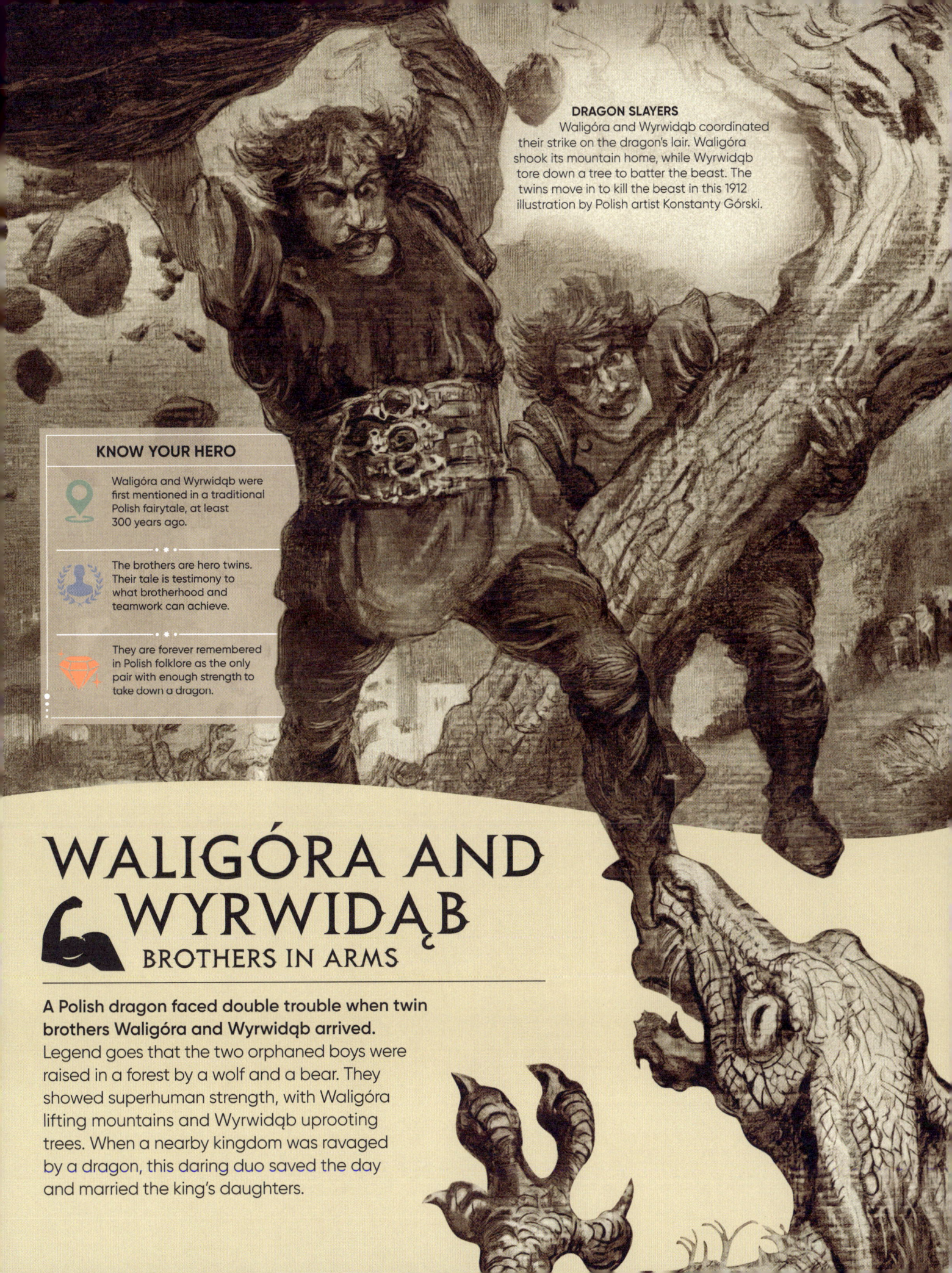

DRAGON SLAYERS
Waligóra and Wyrwidąb coordinated their strike on the dragon's lair. Waligóra shook its mountain home, while Wyrwidąb tore down a tree to batter the beast. The twins move in to kill the beast in this 1912 illustration by Polish artist Konstanty Górski.

KNOW YOUR HERO

Waligóra and Wyrwidąb were first mentioned in a traditional Polish fairytale, at least 300 years ago.

The brothers are hero twins. Their tale is testimony to what brotherhood and teamwork can achieve.

They are forever remembered in Polish folklore as the only pair with enough strength to take down a dragon.

WALIGÓRA AND WYRWIDĄB
BROTHERS IN ARMS

A Polish dragon faced double trouble when twin brothers Waligóra and Wyrwidąb arrived.
Legend goes that the two orphaned boys were raised in a forest by a wolf and a bear. They showed superhuman strength, with Waligóra lifting mountains and Wyrwidąb uprooting trees. When a nearby kingdom was ravaged by a dragon, this daring duo saved the day and married the king's daughters.

Japan's
Megijima Island
is said to be
the location of
Onigashima.

The souls of the vanquished oni rise up into the air.

FRIENDS IN UNLIKELY PLACES
On his way to Onigashima, Momotarō came across three animals – a dog, a monkey, and a pheasant. In exchange for their help in defeating the oni, Momotarō offered each of them *kibi dango* – millet dumplings that his mother had packed for the journey. The creatures happily joined him on his quest.

MOMOTARŌ
DESTROYER OF ONI

Momotarō lived a fabled life, from a magical birth inside a peach to his destiny as the unrivalled champion of his village in Japan.

A loving childhood and the moral values that his parents taught him helped Momotarō grow up to become a strong, courageous, noble, and kind-hearted warrior. When his village was threatened by a band of marauding oni (ogres), Momotarō journeyed to Onigashima ("ogre island") to vanquish them once and for all. He returned home to a hero's welcome, and the treasures he seized from the oni helped his family lead a happy life.

ONI

Giant, ogre-like creatures called oni often appear in Japanese folklore. While most of them live in hell, there are many that walk among humans. Oni are demonic in nature and have animal-like features, such as horns, claws, and sharp teeth. Armed with magical powers, they create chaos on Earth, looting and killing anyone who dares cross them.

DEFEATING THE ONI

When he finally reached Onigashima, Momotarō challenged the oni to a fight. The young warrior and his companions pummelled the oni until they begged for mercy. Momotarō then scatters roasted soybeans to drive away the oni for good in this mid-19th century woodblock print of the scene from a kabuki play on Momotarō.

PEACH BOY

When an elderly, childless couple found a giant peach, little did they know that their lives were about to change for ever. They cut open the fruit to eat it, but to their surprise, a baby boy emerged from within. They named him Momotarō ("peach boy").

KNOW YOUR HERO

Tales of Momotarō come from Japanese folklore, and were first written down in the Edo Period (1603–1868).

Momotarō is a child hero who grew up to become a brave, strong warrior.

He is known for his valiant quest to defeat the ferocious oni (ogres) that had terrorized his land.

PEGASUS
In this painting, Italian artist Fortunino Matania pictures the Greek hero Bellerophon (see p.44) riding the winged horse Pegasus. The hero's steed was the son of the gorgon Medusa and Poseidon, the Greek god of the sea. Pegasus was swift on land and in the skies. The horse was Bellerophon's trusted companion on many adventures, including his ill-fated attempt at reaching Olympus, home of the gods, which ended in the hero's untimely death.

Even though Odysseus wore a disguise, old Argos recognized his master instantly.

ARGOS
When the Greek hero Odysseus (see pp.104–105) set sail for the Trojan War, his dog Argos was just a pup. When Odysseus returned home after 20 years disguised as a beggar, his family didn't recognize him. But Argos knew exactly who he was – the loyal dog recognized his master's footsteps.

BRAN AND SCEÓLANG
Legendary Irish warrior Fionn Mac Cumhaill (see p.75) had two hounds: Bran and Sceólang. They were clever, good at hunting, and fiercely loyal to their master. The hounds also protected Fionn's family – they saved his wife Sadhbh from wolves when she was transformed into a deer, and guarded Fionn's son on hunts.

RAKHSH

When Rostam's father wanted to give him a horse, the Persian hero chose one that no warrior had been able to tame. Rostam used his lasso to capture the horse, and named him Rakhsh ("thunder"). The animal was fast, strong as an elephant, and brave – he once fought and killed a lion (see p.72) to save his master.

LADY TRIỆU'S ELEPHANT

Vietnamese hero Lady Triệu Thị Trinh led a rebellion against a Chinese army (see p.90) from the back of her favourite war elephant. Before this fierce creature became her companion, it roamed freely, terrorizing villages. Lady Triệu was able to tame the wild beast by drawing it into a swamp and climbing onto its head.

ANIMAL ALLIES

Animals are more than just cute sidekicks – from acting as guides to defending their companions, many animals have helped legendary heroes on their adventures.

From small birds to enormous elephants, animal allies are fiercely loyal and their bravery often matches that of the human heroes they accompany. They fearlessly defend them from their foes, sometimes even laying down their own lives to save them from mortal danger.

Yatagarasu's **three legs** represent heaven, earth, and humanity.

The huge bird usually perched on Jimmu's staff.

YATAGARASU

A three-legged crow called Yatagarasu was sent by the gods to guide Emperor Jimmu on his journey to unify Japan (see pp.30–31). It helped Jimmu when he was lost, guiding him through the mountains of Kumano to Yamato, where Jimmu founded a city now known as Kashihara.

SHADI AND BHANUR

Punjabi folk hero Raja Rasalu (see p.157) had two loyal animals: a horse called Bhanur and a parrot named Shadi. They kept him company when he was a child, shut away in an underground palace in Sialkot (in modern-day Pakistan). When he broke free from his prison, they came with him on his adventures.

SHOOTING THE SUNS
There were 10 Suns in the ancient skies. They took turns to shine, scorching the world. One day, when all of them appeared together, Hou Yi shot down all but one, becoming Earth's saviour.

Hou Yi's bow was made of **tiger bone**.

HOU YI
SUN SLAYER

Hou Yi was such a sharp shooter that his arrows never missed their targets – even if he aimed for the Sun!

Hou Yi became famous throughout the country for his incredible skill with the bow and arrow. This brave and generous warrior used his magical bow to protect humans – by shooting down nine Suns and slaying dangerous beasts. Long after his death, he was made into a god himself – Hou Yi, the Chinese god of archery.

Illustration of Hou Yi by Chinese artist Xiao Yuncong, made in the 17th century

KNOW YOUR HERO

Hou Yi's story comes from ancient China and dates back to at least 2000 BCE.

He won the title Lord Archer for his superhuman skill with a bow and arrow.

Hou Yi is famous for his feats of archery, including shooting the Suns and killing monsters.

LEGENDS OF THE SUN
Tales about the Sun appear all over the world. Surya is the Sun god in Hinduism, and in ancient Egypt, the Sun god was called Ra. The Egyptians believed he travelled across the sky from dawn to dusk in a boat. This artefact from ancient Egypt shows a man named Aafenmut (right) offering incense to the seated Sun god, who is pictured as a mummy with the head of a falcon.

Chang'e bids farewell to her husband as she floats up to the Moon.

MOON GODDESS
For shooting down the nine Suns, Hou Yi was rewarded with the Elixir of Immortality, a magical potion that granted eternal life. When one of his students tried to steal it, his wife Chang'e drank the elixir. In one version of her tale, she became so light that she floated to the Moon, becoming the Moon goddess. China's Mid-Autumn Festival at harvest time has celebrated her for over 3,000 years.

THE CHILDREN OF THE SUN
The nine Suns that Hou Yi shot were the children of the Jade Emperor and the Sun Goddess. They fell to the ground in the form of three-legged crows. A single three-legged crow survives inside the one Sun in the sky today.

BOCHICA
TRUE TEACHER

Wise Bochica arrived from the east to show the Muisca people how to live well and in harmony with nature.

A long time ago, bearded Bochica met the Indigenous Muisca people who live in what is now Colombia. He taught them how to farm, spin wool into thread, weave blankets, make pottery, and paint fabric. Bochica's lessons weren't just practical – he also educated the Muisca on how to treat each other well and create a just and flourishing society. When his work was done, he left them to continue to follow his good example.

KNOW YOUR HERO

Bochica is known from the folklore of the Indigenous Muisca people of present-day Colombia in South America.

He taught the people how to behave morally. The Muisca consider him to be a god.

Bochica is famous for teaching them farming, crafts, and how to live together.

GREAT CASCADE
When an angry Muisca god created a flood, the water became trapped on land. Bochica appeared in a rainbow, and struck a rock with his golden staff. This released the floodwaters in a great cascade, forming Colombia's Tequendama waterfall.

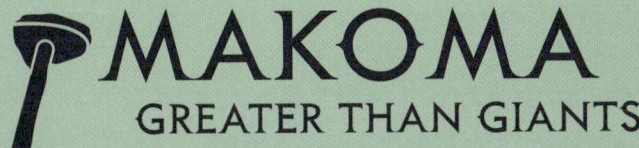 MAKOMA
GREATER THAN GIANTS

With a sack on his shoulder and a hammer in his hand, Makoma defeated every giant he came across – until he met his final foe.

Makoma's iron hammer was a potent weapon, which he used to overcome dangerous giants that roamed the land along the River Zambezi in southern Africa. He would strike them with his hammer, then load them into a sack. Putting the giants in the sack allowed Makoma to take on their supernatural powers to create mountains, rivers, forests, and fire.

KNOW YOUR HERO

 Makoma is known from the stories of the Senna people of Zimbabwe.

 He was incredibly tall and strong – his name means "greater".

 Makoma is famous for defeating giants and acquiring their abilities.

As a child, Makoma killed deadly crocodiles to save his people.

BATTLING A GIANT
Makoma's ancestors ordered him to fight his toughest-ever adversary – a five-headed giant called Sakatirina. This giant was incredibly tall, with legs like mountains. He was so strong that Makoma's blows felt like mere scratches to him. The pair fought for two days before passing out from exhaustion, ending the fight in a draw.

A 1905 illustration by British artist Henry Justice Ford shows the giant holding Makoma in his hands.

YU THE GREAT
TAMER OF THE FLOOD

KNOW YOUR HERO

- Yu the Great appears in myths from ancient China.
- This heroic engineer designed irrigation systems to control flood waters.
- He saved China from terrible floods and founded its first dynasty.

When ancient China faced a great flood 4,000 years ago, only one man stood in the way of the raging waters: a hero named Yu. Yu was born miraculously from the stomach of his dead father and grew up to be a skilled engineer. When wave after wave of water burst the banks of the Yellow River and flowed over the land, Yu worked tirelessly to save his country. He dug a system of ditches, redirecting the water to the sea and saving his people. No wonder the grateful emperor made Yu his heir.

Yu took 13 years to dig all the ditches.

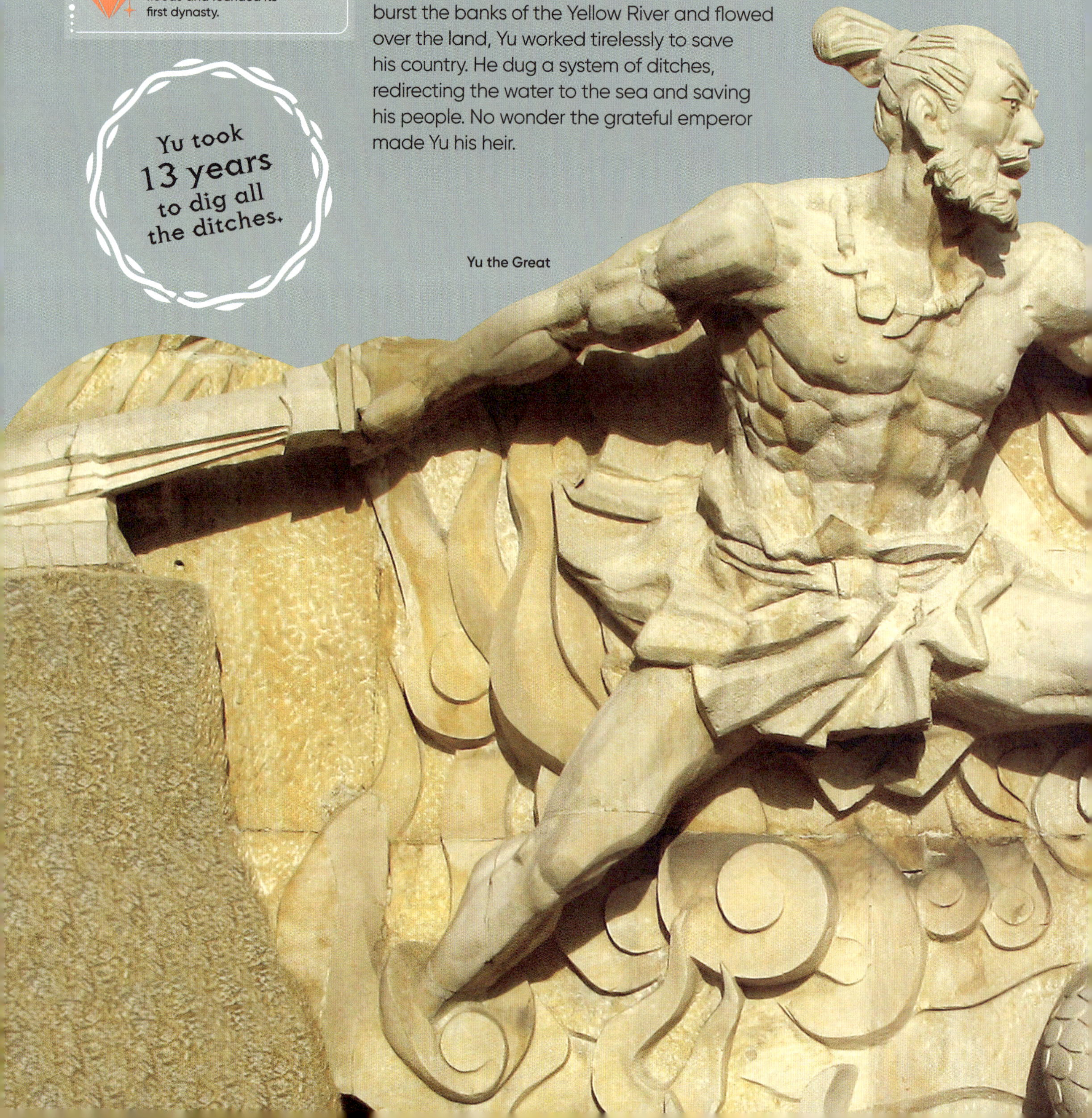

Yu the Great

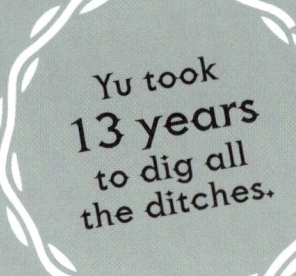

BRILLIANT BUILDERS
Ancient Chinese engineers built a number of significant projects similar to Yu's ditches. In the 3rd century BCE, during the reign of Emperor Qin Shi Huang (left), engineers built the Great Wall of China as well as roads, canals, and a vast royal tomb filled with an army of terracotta statues.

EPIC CONFLICT
Brave and resilient Yu fought and defeated the water god Gonggong and his serpent minister Xiangliu, who were responsible for unleashing the flood. The epic battle can be seen on this marble wall carving at the Dayu Myth Park in Wuhan, China.

ANIMAL AID
Yu didn't battle the floods alone – he was assisted by several animals. One of these helpers was a bixi turtle, as seen here in a temple in China. With the body of a dragon and the shell of a turtle, it was strong enough to move mountains.

Gonggong in his serpent form

MOREMI AJASORO
SPY QUEEN

Queen Moremi Ajasoro of the Yoruba risked it all to save her kingdom and defend her people.

The Yoruba kingdom of Ile-Ife (part of present-day Nigeria) was under constant attack by the forest-dwelling Ìgbò people, who would imprison and enslave the Yoruba. Moremi bravely allowed herself to be captured in order to learn about her enemy's weaknesses. This later helped her to end the Ìgbò's raids and defeat them in battle.

Moremi Statue of Liberty in Osun, Nigeria, built in 2016

A FIERY SOLUTION
After Moremi was captured, she found out that the Ìgbò were covering themselves with dry raffia palm leaves to scare the Yoruba during their raids. She escaped and took this knowledge back to Ile-Ife. She asked the Yoruba people to fight off their attackers with flaming torches so that the leaves could be set ablaze, killing the raiders.

REMEMBERING MOREMI
The legend of Queen Moremi has been passed down through generations. Her bravery and sacrifice are celebrated in poems, songs, and musicals. She is also honoured in traditional Yoruba festivals such as the Olojo festival (above), held every year in Ile-Ife.

KNOW YOUR HERO

 Moremi Ajasoro is known from 12th-century Yoruba stories, which come from the part of Africa that is now Nigeria.

 She was a princess of the Yoruba people and married the king of Ile-Ife.

 Moremi is honoured for freeing the Yoruba from Ìgbò attacks and sacrificing her son as the price for victory.

The Edi festival celebrates Moremi with feasting over seven days.

KNOW YOUR HERO

Köroğlu is first mentioned in the 17th-century *Seyahatname* ("Book of Travels") by Ottoman Turkish explorer Evliya Çelebi.

 This folk hero from Central Asia was as skilled at riding a horse as he was at playing music.

 Köroğlu is famous for fighting back against an unjust society.

КОРОГЛУ илл. А.ГАДЖИЕВА

10 к 1989 ПОЧТА CCCP

Russian stamp from 1989 shows Köroğlu riding his horse.

HORSE AND COMPANION
Köroğlu was an expert horse rider – a skill he had learned from his father, a horse trainer. Köroğlu and his brave steed Kirat rode together into many battles and adventures.

KÖROĞLU
REBEL MINSTREL

The Central Asian folk hero Köroğlu fought for the downtrodden and was a symbol of justice for many.

When Köroğlu was just a boy, his father was blinded by a cruel ruler. This act made a big impression on Köroğlu – he grew up determined to take revenge. In time, he became driven to act against injustice, riding out from his mountain lair to fight unjust rulers, rob the rich, and help the poor. This mounted warrior was also a skilled minstrel who could draw people to him with his beautiful music.

Köroğlu played the *çöğür*, a musical instrument like a lute.

ANGABO
CLEVER KING

Angabo's brains and bravery turned him from a humble peasant into a king.
Legend has it that a fierce dragonlike serpent called Arwe terrorized the African territory of Ethiopia for 400 years. It was Angabo who came up with a clever way of killing this monster – by feeding it a poisoned goat. Celebrated across Ethiopia, Angabo became its first king, followed by his daughter Makeda, Queen of Sheba.

KNOW YOUR HERO

- Angabo appears in Ethiopia's lists of kings, first written down in the 13th century CE.
- He became king of Ethiopia and founded a mighty empire in the 14th century BCE.
- He is famous for killing a terrible serpent.

Some historians believe Angabo founded the Ag'azyan Dynasty.

KILLING THE BEAST
When Angabo saw people forced to worship the giant snake and offer it human and animal sacrifices, he knew what to do. Mixing poison from a euphorbia tree into a potion, he fed it to his goat and gave the goat to Arwe. Angabo's triumph is shown in this section from a 16th-century Ethiopian fresco.

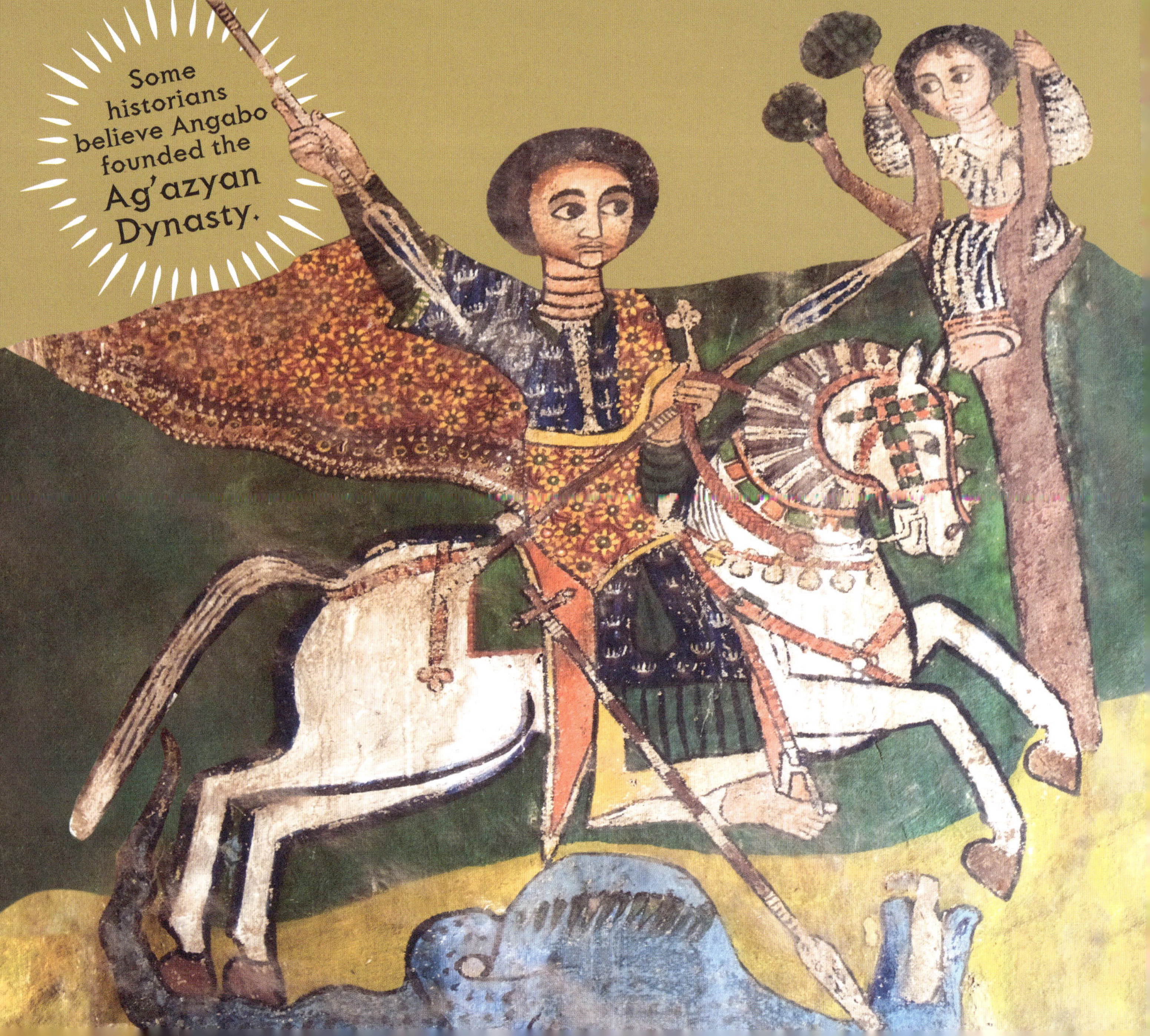

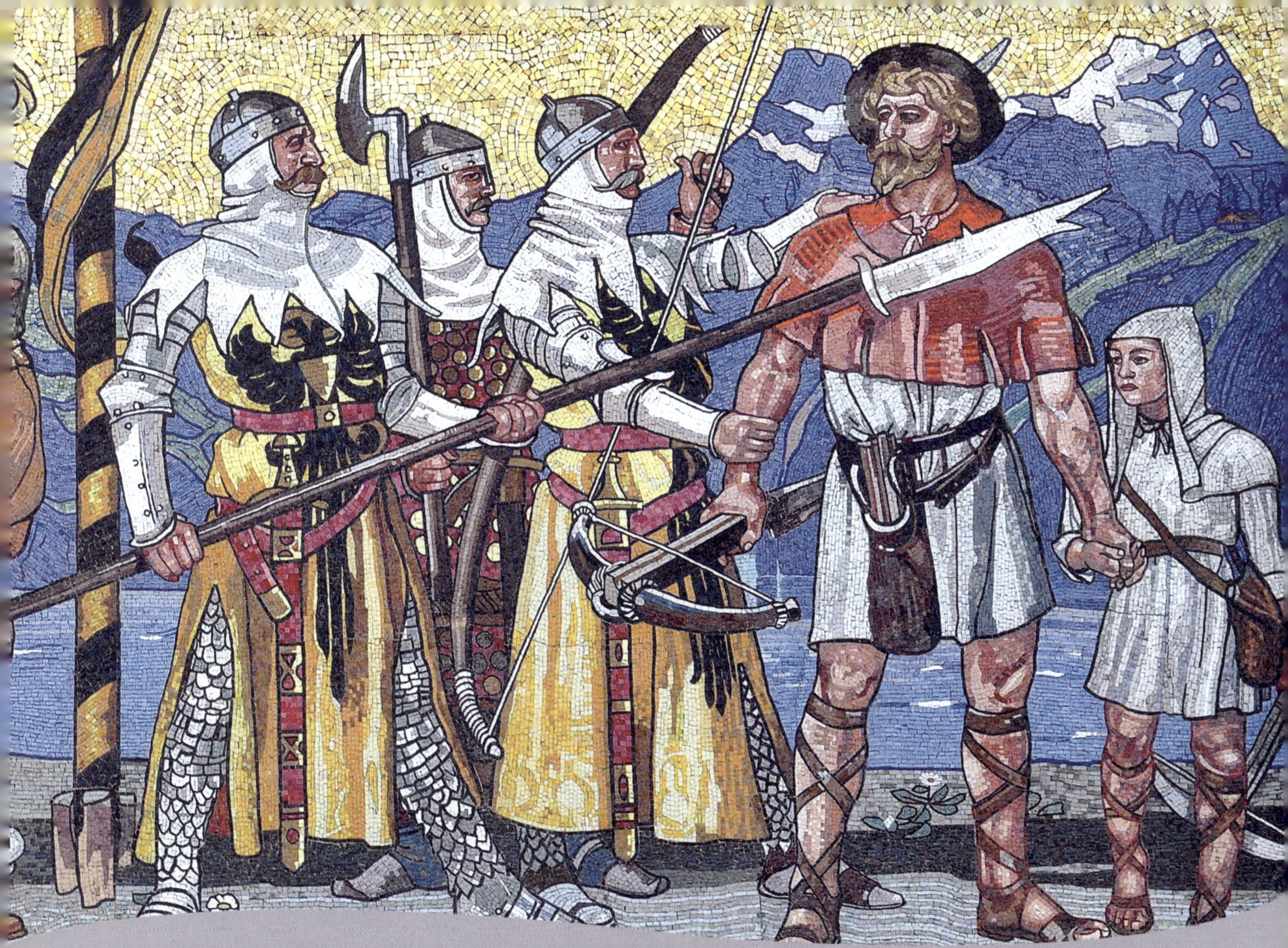

WILLIAM TELL

SHARP SHOOTER

Swiss folk hero William Tell was a highly skilled marksman, able to send a bolt from his crossbow into nearly any target.

William Tell's beloved country Switzerland was suffering under Austrian rule in the 14th century. The local Austrian governor Albrecht Gessler was a cruel man. When Tell refused to obey Gessler's commands, he was arrested and threatened with execution. Tell's defiance has inspired the Swiss people and many others to fight for their freedom down through the centuries.

A TEST OF ACCURACY

As punishment for his defiance, Tell was ordered to shoot an apple off his son's head. Tell managed the task, but he was furious that his son had been put in danger. He had planned to use a second crossbow bolt on the governor if his son died.

KNOW YOUR HERO

William Tell appears in 15th-century folk stories from Switzerland.

He was an incredible marksman, skilled with a crossbow.

Tell is famous for shooting an apple off his son's head and resisting tyranny.

CROSSING THE TIBER
Cloelia had to lead the hostages across the raging waters of the Tiber, under a hail of Etruscan javelins. In this 16th-century print by Italian artist Giulio di Antonio Bonasone, she crosses on horseback, with the others preparing to swim behind her.

THE SIEGE OF ROME
Before Rome became a mighty empire, it was a small city-state, in frequent conflict with its neighbours. Rome was even ruled by Etruscan kings for a time. The Siege of Rome in 508 BCE saw Rome surrounded by Etruscan armies and on the brink of war.

CLOELIA
LEGENDARY LIBERATOR

Noble Cloelia led captured Roman women out of an enemy camp.
A peace treaty ended the Etruscan siege of Rome in 508 BCE, but in exchange, Cloelia and a group of Roman women were taken as hostages by the Etruscans. She led the women in a daring escape across the River Tiber while dodging enemy fire. The Romans forced the group to go back to maintain the treaty, but Cloelia's bravery impressed the Etruscans enough to let some hostages go free.

KNOW YOUR HERO

Cloelia appears in tales of ancient Rome recorded by the historian Livy in the 1st century BCE.

She was a Roman woman who showed great bravery after she was captured by Etruscan king Lars Porsena.

This legendary woman is known for leading a group of Roman hostages to safety.

RAJA RASALU
PROTECTOR OF PUNJAB

Prince Rasalu killed giants, defeated a cruel king, and became one of the legendary monarchs of the Punjab region in India and Pakistan.
Rasalu grew up alone in an underground palace, but became an excellent warrior, skilled in many weapons. At the age of 11, he set out to explore the world. He slayed giants preying on a town, stopped a king from killing innocent people, and rescued animals in peril. He went on to become the ruler of the kingdom of Sialkot (now in Pakistan). To this day, he is known as Raja Rasalu (King Rasalu).

A GAME OF DICE
A king named Sarkap liked to play *chaupar* (a board game) with enchanted dice – after winning, he would kill his opponent. Eager to stop him, Rasalu challenged him to a game, but swapped out the dice with his own. Rasalu won easily and made Sarkap promise to stop killing other players, putting an end to the king's tyranny.

KNOW YOUR HERO

 Raja Rasalu features in Punjabi folktales from South Asia that were written down in the 19th century.

 He is known as a warrior, a champion of the people, and a protector of animals.

 He famously killed a group of giants to protect the town of Nila.

CLOSE COMPANIONS
Born to the queen of Sialkot but forbidden from seeing his parents, Rasalu travelled far and wide. As seen in this 19th-century manuscript printed in Lahore, Pakistan, he was accompanied by two companions: a horse called Bhanur and a parrot called Shadi.

ARCHER'S AMBUSH
When falsely accused of hunting royal deer, Robin Hood retreated into the leafy undergrowth of Sherwood Forest to avoid capture. From high up on tree branches, he would ambush the sheriff's procession outside Nottingham Castle, as shown by English artist James Edwin McConnell.

ROBIN HOOD
BIG-HEARTED BANDIT

The hero Robin Hood risked life and limb to rob from the rich and give to the poor, making him popular in English folklore.

Robin Hood was a skilled archer who always stayed one step ahead of his evil enemy, the sheriff of Nottingham. The selfish sheriff raised taxes so high that people were left homeless, while stockpiling the money for himself. To put an end to the tyranny of the sheriff and other nobles, Robin Hood and his loyal band of local outlaws – called the Merry Men – began stealing for those in need. His desire to protect the poor made him a true champion of the people.

DEFIANT OUTLAWS
Outlaws are lawbreakers who avoid punishment by hiding from the authorities. In medieval Europe, many outlaws stole from the rich to survive. Slovakia's answer to Robin Hood was the outlaw Juraj Jánošík, who rode around robbing the rich.

KNOW YOUR HERO

 The legend of Robin Hood hails from medieval England during the 13th–14th centuries.

 Both folk hero and thieving outlaw, Robin Hood stars in many retellings from medieval ballads to Hollywood blockbusters.

 He and his men famously robbed the rich to feed the poor – aided by Maid Marian in some versions of the tale.

Robin Hood's green clothing helped **camouflage** *him in the forest.*

FROM FOE TO FRIEND
Legend has it that Robin Hood met a man named Little John on a narrow bridge. Neither would back down to let the other pass, so they battled each other. While Robin was a good fighter, Little John matched him blow for blow and eventually knocked Robin into the river. Impressed by Little John's strength, Robin Hood invited him to join his Merry Men.

Little John

Robin Hood

The two men fought using long wooden sticks known as quarterstaves.

BUILDING THE RAILWAYS

The railways helped the expansion of the US, with settlements springing up along the routes across the country. Work was difficult and dangerous, and many workers, especially Black and Chinese people, died in the poor conditions. The invention of new machinery such as steam drills made work quicker, but it also took jobs away from people who needed them.

KNOW YOUR HERO

 John Henry is known from African American folklore in the US. His story dates back to a folk ballad set in the 1870s, after the American Civil War.

 He is a folk hero, famous for his strength and determination. He could work for hours without rest.

 John Henry achieved a mighty feat of strength, working faster than a steam drill to prove that people were better than machines.

JOHN HENRY
HAMMER WIELDER

Which is mightier, human or machine? John Henry took on a steam drill in a head-to-head competition.

Stories among Black people of the US gave rise to the legend of John Henry. In the 19th century, steam drills were being used to make tunnels for the new railways. John Henry took on the machine, and attacked the rock furiously with a heavy hammer in each hand. Henry won, but died from the enormous effort.

Each hammer was made of steel.

John Henry worked with a pair of **10-pound** hammers.

RISING TO THE CHALLENGE

John Henry proved man's superior power during the construction of a railway tunnel in West Virginia in the 1870s. This book illustration by US artist Jerry Pinkney in 1994 shows him hard at work with two hammers.

JOE MAGARAC
STEEL MAKER

Made of steel and 2 m (7 ft) tall with hands the size of buckets, Joe Magarac was an extraordinary man with a single purpose: to make steel. Joe's tall tale comes from the folktales of steelworkers in Pennsylvania, US. He was a hero to his fellow workers, and saved many of them from accidents. He made more steel than his factory could sell, and then melted himself down to create even more.

SUPERHUMAN SKILL
Joe Magarac could work at a rate unmatched by any ordinary human, labouring for 24 hours straight without a break. In this illustration by German artist Lisa Bolur, he grabs red-hot molten steel with his bare hands.

Joe Magarac carried his lunch in a **washtub**.

KNOW YOUR HERO

Joe Magarac features in stories from Pennsylvania, US, dating back to the 1930s.

Born in a mine, this folk hero was called the Genie of Steel for his superhuman feats as a steelworker.

Magarac is famous for rescuing his fellow workers from a runaway train.

PAUL BUNYAN
LUMBER LEGEND

Unusually tall and strong, Paul Bunyan was a giant who worked as a lumberjack, chopping down trees in Canada and the US. Paul was enormous from the day he was born – instead of the one stork that traditionally brings a new baby, it took five to carry Paul. He became so big that just rolling over in his sleep caused an earthquake. One day he found a blue baby ox stuck in the snow. He named it Babe, and over time it grew huge. Paul and Babe worked quickly, clearing far more trees than anyone else could ever hope to, and reshaping entire landscapes.

FLATTENING THE LAND
Paul cut down millions of trees to create what are now the US states of North and South Dakota. He hammered the tree stumps into the ground and made the land as flat as a board – and perfect for farming.

BATTLE FOR THE AXE
Two teams, the Minnesota Golden Gophers and the Wisconsin Badgers, have one of US college football's longest rivalries. When they play against each other, the winning team receives a trophy that is modelled after Paul Bunyan's giant axe.

Paul's daily diet included two dozen eggs.

Babe hauled logs, wagons, and this huge plough to clear whole forests.

CHANGING THE LANDSCAPE
Paul and Babe left their mark across North America. In the state of Washington, they made the huge estuary known as Puget Sound with their plough. In Minnesota, their giant footprints created 10,000 lakes. And it was Paul who carved out the Grand Canyon by dragging his giant axe behind him.

KNOW YOUR HERO

Paul Bunyan comes from the oral folklore of North American loggers in the 19th century. His stories became hugely popular thanks to a 1922 book by William B Laughead.

He is a lumberjack – someone who cuts down trees for their wood.

Paul is famous for his enormous size and strength, and his gigantic ox Babe.

TOWERING LUMBERJACK

When the first Paul Bunyan stories were published in 1910, he was said to be 2 m (7 ft) tall. But as his cult status grew, so did he – by the 1920s, he towered over trees. In 1996, the United States Postal Service issued this postage stamp to celebrate the folk hero and his big blue ox.

Paul's axe was enormous, to match its massive owner.

32 USA

PAUL BUNYAN

1996

MAGICIANS AND TRICKSTERS

Not all heroes are as they seem. Some were blessed with magical powers, which helped them dazzle and defeat their foes. From spell-casting to shapeshifting, these special skills enabled them to save the day when everyone least expected it.

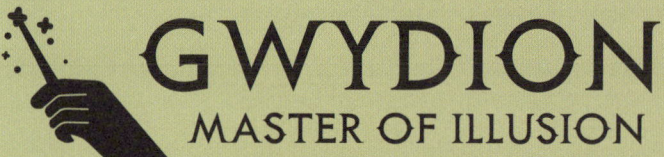

GWYDION
MASTER OF ILLUSION

The sorcerer Gwydion's magic weaves through ancient Welsh mythology.

Cunning and clever, this son of the goddess Dôn could conjure marvellous illusions to fool people, sometimes for his own greed and gains. Gwydion tricked his longstanding rival Pryderi, the king of Dyfed, into giving him his magical pigs. Pryderi was furious when he found out, but Gwydion had already vanished. The pair went head to head on the battlefield, resulting in Gwydion finally killing Pryderi.

KNOW YOUR HERO

This trickster magician first appeared in *The Mabinogion*, a collection of early Welsh tales taken from oral tradition.

Gwydion used his magic powers to shapeshift into animals, turn trees into warriors, and defeat his enemies.

A skilled warrior, Gwydion defeated his rival Pryderi in an epic contest that tested his magic and fighting skills.

WELSH WIZARDRY
In this 1984 illustration, Welsh artist Margaret Jones shows Gwydion conjuring up 12 hounds and 12 horses from toadstools to give Pryderi in exchange for his pigs. When these fake gifts turned back into toadstools, Pryderi was outraged.

The golden chariot was pulled by serpents.

LUCKY ESCAPE
Using her knowledge of potions, Medea poisoned Jason's new bride in revenge for his betrayal. Afterwards, she fled from Corinth to Athens on a golden chariot sent by her grandfather Helios – as seen in this Greek vase painting from 400 BCE.

MEDEA
ENCHANTING SORCERESS

Medea could make almost anyone fall under her spell in ancient Greek mythology, but if they didn't, she unleashed the full force of her magic. The granddaughter of the Sun god Helios, Medea was born with divine powers, including the ability to see the future and create potent potions. She helped the hero Jason obtain the Golden Fleece by protecting him with her magic and vanquishing his enemies with powerful spells. But when he left her for another woman, she sought revenge.

KNOW YOUR HERO

Medea, princess of Colchis, was first mentioned by the ancient Greek writer Hesiod in c.700 BCE.

Her divine origins gave her magical abilities. She became a powerful sorceress.

She is best known for assisting the hero Jason in his quest to take the Golden Fleece.

TSUNADE
SLUG WIELDER

Japan's young slug-wielding warrior Tsunade was a hero like no other.

When Tsunade's clan was attacked by a ninja warrior and serpent sorcerer named Orochimaru, she took revenge. A master magician had taught her powerful magic performed with slugs, and she used this gift on the battlefield, countering the ninja's snake magic and restoring her clan.

Among, Tsunade's many magical talents was **walking on water.**

KNOW YOUR HERO

Tsunade found fame in Japanese folklore from the 18th century.

This folk hero was an expert in slug magic and healed her allies.

She successfully used her magic to counter Orochimaru's snake venom.

AMAZING ANTIDOTE
Tsunade could summon a supersized slug – as shown in this 19th-century woodblock print – or even shapeshift into one. Her slug magic was the only antidote to Orochimaru's venom when he took the form of a serpent. Tsunade went on to join forces with the hero Jiraiya in his battle with the ninja.

JIRAIYA
TOAD RIDER

The Japanese folk hero Jiraiya used all his skills in magic and martial arts to defeat his archenemy, the serpent sorcerer Orochimaru.

Jiraiya was already a master of martial arts and swordfighting when he was taught magic by a shapeshifting toad. He learned to summon toads and use their mystical powers to defeat his enemies and defend the poor. When Orochimaru robbed him, Jiraiya used magic to defeat the ninja – aided by Tsunade, who had magic powers of her own.

The name Jiraiya means "young thunder" in Japanese.

TOAD TROUBLE
When Jiraiya tried to rob a shapeshifting toad, he failed. But instead of punishing him, the toad taught him magic. Jiraiya could now summon giant toads, as seen in this 1852 woodblock print by Japanese artist Utagawa Kunisada.

MWINDO
MIRACULOUS CHILD

The name Mwindo has a special place in the tales of the Nyanga people of Central and East Africa.

According to the *Epic of Mwindo*, he was a child with supernatural powers who was born fully grown and holding a conga sceptre (magical fly swatter). His father, Chief Shemwindo, feared losing his kingdom to his son, so he tried countless times to kill him, but Mwindo's magic protected him against every attack. He led a life of breathtaking adventure – slaying a dragon, travelling to the underworld, and becoming a great leader.

KNOW YOUR HERO

 Mwindo's story spread by word of mouth among the Nyanga people, but as it was not written down, its exact origins are unknown.

 He is hailed as a hero in Nyanga oral folklore for his powers and for his able leadership.

 Mwindo stands out for his magical powers and his ability to outsmart his foes.

RETELLING STORIES
Although many oral stories from Africa have been written down for everyone to read, they were originally only spoken aloud or performed in song and dance at local gatherings. Today, the *Epic of Mwindo* (left) and similar stories are still acted out in dramatic performances. According to Kenyan folklore, performers starring in this particular epic receive protection against death.

SUPERHUMAN STRENGTH
Born with prodigious strength, quick thinking, and magical powers, Mwindo was invincible. His conga sceptre could block any weapon, from spears to lightning bolts. On top of that, his uncles were blacksmiths – they took Mwindo to pieces, and used fire to forge them into a body of iron. Nothing could harm him.

Mwindo's scepter was made from a **buffalo tail** on a wooden handle.

No weapon could pierce Mwindo's iron body.

HILDR
SAVIOUR OF THE FALLEN

The only chance of revival for slain heroes in Norse mythology came in the form of Princess Hildr.

Hildr was torn between her loyalty to her father King Högni and her love for her suitor Prince Heðinn. When Heðinn killed Hildr's mother, King Högni went to war against him. Hildr wished to prevent further bloodshed, so she used magic to revive dead warriors on both sides every day – setting them up for a never-ending battle. In Old Norse, Hildr's name means "battle".

AGENT OF ODIN

The name Hildr is linked to the dead in Norse mythology. Among the god Odin's band of immortal female warriors was a valkyrie named Hildr. She carried the souls of warriors who had died in battle to Valhalla, the home of fallen heroes.

PROSE EDDA

In the 13th century, Icelandic author Snorri Sturluson wrote one of the most important books in Norse history. The *Prose Edda* recounts Norse myths and legends in detail. The title page shown here is taken from an 18th-century version of the book.

EVERLASTING BATTLE

The Norse battle of Heodening raged between the rival armies of King Högni and Prince Heðinn. Hildr brought their dead soldiers back to life every night, as seen in this Viking picture stone from the 7th century CE. The armies fought at full strength again the next day, in an endless cycle of conflict.

The armies battle each other in this scene, with Hildr caught in the middle.

KNOW YOUR HERO

 The story of Hildr was first written in the 9th-century poem *Ragnarsdrápa* ("Ragnar's Poem").

 This death-defying princess is King Högni's daughter and a skilled magician.

 She is known for her magical power to revive the dead.

ALADDIN
PEASANT PRINCE

The rags-to-riches story of Aladdin reads like a fairy tale in which a young boy finds a magical way to make his dreams come true. Aladdin's courage and quick thinking helped him overcome deadly obstacles, while his generosity and kindness captured many hearts. Faced with an evil magician masquerading as his uncle, Aladdin refused to give in to his demands and outwitted him at every turn. The accidental discovery of a magic lamp that held a powerful wish-granting genie transformed his life, allowing him to help people and do good in the world. While Aladdin's tale is likely set in Southwest Asia, his legend has spread far and wide.

CAUGHT IN A TRAP
A ghastly magician pretending to be Aladdin's uncle sent the young boy into a gloomy cave to retrieve a golden lamp. Aladdin found the lamp, but refused to hand it over until he was allowed out. Although the magician shut him inside the cave, Aladdin later managed to escape.

GRANTING WISHES
When Aladdin rubbed the lamp with his hands, a genie appeared, promising to make his wishes come true. Aladdin went on to get everything he asked for, including a spectacular palace and a princess bride.

The word "genie" comes from the French word "génie".

TRANSLATED TALES
It is often said that the story of Aladdin comes from an Arabic collection of folk tales called *Alf layla wa-layla* ("One Thousand and One Nights"). However, it was first told by a Syrian storyteller named Hanna Diyab. French author Antoine Galland was the first European to translate it, in his 18th-century French version of the Arabic collection.

LES
MILLE ET UNE NUIT,
CONTES ARABES,
TRADUITS EN FRANÇOIS
PAR M. GALLAND.
NOUVELLE ÉDITION CORRIGÉE;
TOME VI.

A PARIS,
PAR LA COMPAGNIE DES LIBRAIRES.

M. DCC. XLV.
Avec Approbation & Privilege du Roi.

In some versions of the story, the genie appears in a human-like form with animal-like features such as horns.

HELPFUL HERO
Aladdin became very wealthy after the genie made many of his wishes come true. But our hero didn't keep his newfound riches to himself. Instead, he rode around town, giving out gold coins to everyone else. His generosity and willingness to share with the people won him their hearts.

MAGIC LAMP
Oil lamps have been used in Southwest Asia for thousands of years. People use them to light up their homes, during festivals, and to pay respects to the dead. Lamps have also featured in folk tales from the region, and often have magical powers. This oil lamp from Syria was made in the 12th century CE.

KNOW YOUR HERO

There are many versions of Aladdin's story, and some are set in Southwest Asia.

He becomes a prince thanks to a magical genie and his own determination.

Aladdin is best known for finding the genie and outwitting an evil sorcerer.

Swept off his feet, the Monkey King fought hard to take the fan.

The banana leaf fan could even put out **volcanoes.**

GOLDEN FLEECE
The Golden Fleece of ancient Greek legend was the woolly coat of a ram. It belonged to a king, Aeëtes, who dedicated it to Ares, the god of war, and hung it up in a grove of trees guarded by a serpent. But Aeëtes' daughter Medea drugged the snake and helped the hero Jason to steal it (see p.120).

BANANA LEAF FAN
Chinese princess Lady Iron Fan owned a magical banana leaf fan, which could put out fires and create heavy gusts of wind. These winds were strong enough to blow her enemies into the air and send them flying far, far away. In this 1868 woodblock print, Japanese artist Tsukioka Yoshitoshi shows her fighting a supernatural character called the Monkey King.

Huge leaf from a banana tree

FLYING CARPET

A magic carpet usually allows its rider to soar high into the air and travel great distances. In one Russian folk tale, the sorceress Baba Yaga lets Ivan use a magic flying carpet to capture the mythical firebird and carry it home in order to win the hand of a princess.

MAGICAL OBJECTS

Many stories about legendary heroes feature objects that are magical or mysterious. These items often play a special role in the hero's story.

Magical objects may be created in unusual circumstances, such as the fish hook made by the Polynesian demigod Māui with his grandmother's help. Many are gifts from the gods, such as the cap of invisibility given to the Greek hero Perseus. Heroes may have to prove themselves worthy of using these extraordinary tools, or fight off those who want to steal them.

CAP OF INVISIBILITY

The Greek hero Perseus was given a cap of invisibility by the god Hades. Wearing it made Perseus impossible to see, so he was able to sneak up on the deadly gorgon Medusa and cut off her head (see p.45).

TE MATAU-A-MĀUI

The Polynesian demigod Māui had a colossal fishhook called Te Matau-a-Māui, which he made from the jawbone of his grandmother. He cast it into the Pacific Ocean and hauled the chain of islands now called Hawai'i up to the surface (see pp.134–135).

CONGA-SCEPTRE

Mwindo, a great leader of the Nyanga people from Central and East Africa, was born holding a fly swatter with a wooden handle and buffalo tail (see p.170). With a wave of the swatter, Mwindo could make food appear and bring people back from the dead. He could send it far away to attack his enemies!

GIANTS

Some cultures describe giants as dimwitted creatures who terrorize humans. But the giants of Norse legends were talented and full of wisdom. In Norse tales, a giant built the wall around the home of the gods. The Norse giants were also skilled warriors who could wield many weapons, like in this Germanic engraving from 1901.

SAN MARTIN TXIKI

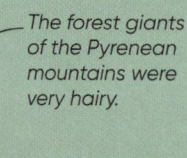

BOY IN BOOTS

Little rascal San Martin Txiki outwitted giants to make a big impact on the lives of the Basque people.
San Martin used his wits to steal the secrets of farming and making tools for the benefit of his people. This clever trickster discovered how to grow wheat, make saws, and solder iron from the forest-dwelling Basajaunak giants, who were farmers and blacksmiths.

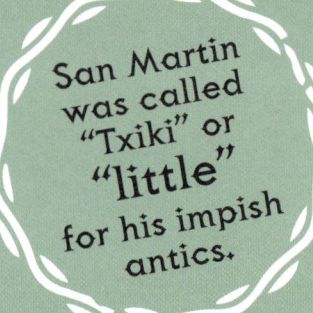

The forest giants of the Pyrenean mountains were very hairy.

San Martin was called "Txiki" or "little" for his impish antics.

KNOW YOUR HERO

San Martin Txiki's tale was first told in the Basque region of France and Spain.

He was a folk hero for the Basque people, giving them key skills for survival.

He tricked the Basajaunak giants into revealing the secrets of farming and toolmaking for his people.

STEALING WHEAT
San Martin Txiki told the Basajaunak he could jump over their wheat more gracefully than them. The giants cleared the jump easily, but the trickster purposefully landed in the wheat. This filled his large boots with grains of wheat, which he carried back to his people.

ALDAR KOSE
SLY MINSTREL

Master of deception Aldar Kose stole the show in Kazakh folklore by singing songs, outwitting the rich, and helping the poor.
Some called Aldar a swindler, but his heart was always in the right place. One icy winter he convinced a wealthy man to swap his fur coat by pretending the many holes in his own tattered coat helped the cold to escape! Another time, he was able to feed a hungry child by tricking a fruit seller. He even sold beans he said would grow into donkeys – they never did.

Aldar Kose strums a musical instrument called a dombra in this 2013 coin from Kazakhstan.

KAZAKH PUPPETRY
Puppet shows have been popular in Kazakhstan for centuries. This tradition evolved when stories were shared by word of mouth and presented to local audiences with puppets acting out the stories. To this day, many puppetry performances retell the tales of Aldar Kose.

SINGING ALONG
Aldar performed as a minstrel, singing songs and strumming his stringed dombra while riding around on a donkey. His performances proved an effective distraction, making it easier for him to trick the wealthy and take their money and possessions.

KNOW YOUR HERO

Stories featuring Aldar Kose have been passed down through oral tradition for centuries, before his story was turned into a play in the 1940s.

His clever tricks and playful mischief make him one of the best-loved Kazakh heroes.

This Kazakh legend deceived the wealthy, tricking them into giving away their possessions for the poor and needy.

KAURAS
GIANT FOOLER

Kauras was a clever young boy who dared to lock horns with a cruel and hideous giant.

Kauras came up with a cunning idea to defeat the giant Stalo, who had been terrorizing the Sámi people of Sápmi in Northern Europe. The young lad tricked Stalo into accepting an unusual contest – head-butting a tree. The winner of the contest would be the one who made the biggest hole in the tree's trunk. When Kauras won, Stalo had to leave, never to return.

A GIANT PROBLEM
Stalo forced the Sámi people to bring him offerings of cheese and meat. If he didn't get enough offerings, he would kill their reindeer, or send wolves to hunt them. Stalo was even known to eat humans – including noisy children at Christmas.

KNOW YOUR HERO

Kauras appears in the folklore of the Sámi people, who live near the Arctic Circle.

This boy hero is known for being brave and quick-witted.

He defeated a giant named Stalo, who had been attacking his homeland.

BUTTING HEADS
Kauras made sure the giant head-butted the tree first – as seen in this illustration from 1904–1908 by Swedish artist John Bauer. Stalo ran at it so hard that he knocked himself out, but made no dent in the tree. While the giant was dazed, Kauras carved a big hole in the tree, then covered it with bark. His own head butt revealed this huge hole, making him seem immensely strong.

SCHEHERAZADE
SEASONED STORYTELLER

Thanks to her clever storytelling, brave Scheherazade managed to outwit the king and save the lives of many women.
Scheherazade was the daughter of the vizier (chief advisor) of King Shahryar, the ruler of a Persian kingdom. Each night, the king would marry a new wife, then have her beheaded in the morning. Scheherazade devised a plan to stop the king, so she offered to marry him. Night after night she kept him entertained with the legends of kings and civilizations, stopping just short of each ending to keep him wanting more. This kept her alive and stopped the king killing more wives.

KNOW YOUR HERO

 Scheherazade stars in the Arabic collection of stories called *One Thousand and One Nights*.

 She was a skilled storyteller, able to enchant listeners with her words.

 She famously survived her marriage to a king who killed all his previous wives.

One Thousand and One Nights is narrated by Scheherazade.

TELLING STORIES
Scheherazade told stories so captivating that King Shahryar listened all night long. At dawn, she would pause the story, promising to finish it the next night. The curious king would spare her life to find out how the story ended. This continued for 1,001 nights, until she had told him 1,000 stories and borne him three children.

Scheherazade and the king in a 20th-century painting by French artist Léon Carré

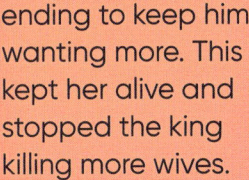

MORGIANA
QUICK THINKER

Brave Morgiana used her brains to outwit her master's enemies, saving his life and winning her freedom.

In a thrilling tale from Southwest Asia, a woodcutter named Ali Baba stole treasure belonging to a band of thieves, which landed him in trouble. The thieves marked his house, hoping to return under the cover of darkness. When Ali Baba's servant Morgiana discovered the plot, she marked all the neighbouring houses in the same way to confuse the villains. Even so, they eventually found Ali Baba's house and snuck inside, hidden in giant jars, to wait for nightfall. But Morgiana saw through this ruse too, and quickly poured boiling oil into each jar, killing the thieves one by one. She had saved her master's life, and Ali Baba was so grateful that he gave Morgiana her freedom.

OPEN SESAME!
Ali Baba found a cave packed full of glittering treasures, which belonged to a band of forty thieves. He entered it by saying the magical words "Open Sesame!", and took some of the treasure for himself. But when the thieves found out that Ali Baba had stolen from them, they decided to kill him.

KNOW YOUR HERO

Morgiana stars in *Ali Baba and the Forty Thieves*, one of the stories in Southwest Asia's *One Thousand and One Nights*.

She was quick-witted, brave, and loyal to her employer.

Morgiana saved Ali Baba from being killed by dangerous thieves.

HIDDEN IN PLAIN SIGHT
The thieves hid in empty oil jars and had them delivered by mule to Ali Baba. This illustration from around 1905–1920 shows clever Morgiana pouring boiling oil into the jars to kill the stowaways.

FRANCISCO EL HOMBRE
MUSICAL MAVERICK

Talented El Hombre could play music so beautifully that anyone who heard it would stop to listen.
Francisco rode from town to town in Colombia on his donkey, carrying news and stories, singing songs, and playing amazing tunes on his accordion. He was an expert musician, and could beat anyone who challenged him to a musical duel. After outplaying the Devil himself, he earned the title of Francisco "El Hombre", or "the man".

KNOW YOUR HERO

 Francisco El Hombre appears in the folklore of Colombia. His legend may have been inspired by musician Francisco Guerra, who was born in 1849.

 He is a skilled musician who plays traditional Colombian music called vallenato.

 El Hombre is famous for playing a musical duel with the Devil, and beating him at his own game.

VALLENATO
Traditional Colombian music, called vallenato, has poetic lyrics and is played on a range of instruments including the accordion, drum, and wire comb. The music is key to preserving Colombia's oral storytelling tradition.

El Hombre was armed with only his accordian when he faced the Devil.

*Colombian musicians still compete in **piquerias** (duels) today.*

DUEL WITH THE DEVIL
One night as Francisco played his accordion, he met the Devil. The villain played dark tunes that made the Moon and stars vanish. But Francisco was able to outduel his opponent, restoring the light of the Moon and stars, and banishing the Devil.

FIND OUT MORE

History has countless tales of legendary heroes, so this book can't cover them all. Here is a glimpse of a few more special heroes from around the world.

AIWEL LONGAR
South Sudan (Dinka people)
The son of a water spirit, Aiwel took charge when his village was plagued by drought. He led his people to a new land with plentiful water where they could thrive again.

SUDIKA-MBAMBI
Angola (Ambundu people)
The child hero Sudika-mbambi battled ogres, visited the underworld, and found himself thrown down a hole. He survived these adventures and more, before taking his place in the sky as thunder.

HEITSI-EIBIB
South Africa, Namibia, Botswana (Khoekhoe people)
A powerful chief, Heitsi-Eibib was a skilled hunter and cunning trickster. Despite dying multiple times, he came back bigger and stronger. After many failed to kill the monster Ga-Gorib, Heitsi-Eibib tricked him and struck him dead from behind with a stone.

LITUOLONE
Lesotho, South Africa (Basotho people)
At birth, Lituolone was already grown up. He and his mother were the only people alive – the ferocious monster Kammapa had eaten everyone else. When Lituolone fought the monster, he was swallowed too. From inside its belly, Lituolone tore Kammapa apart, releasing the people that had been eaten.

SUIRENSHI
China
While out in the forest, a curious Suirenshi rubbed two sticks together and made fire. He shared his groundbreaking discovery with all his people, transforming their lives for the better with warmth, light, and a way to cook food.

JI GONG
China
When Ji Gong was a young man, he chose to join a monastery and become a Buddhist monk. Selfless by nature, he went to great lengths to help the poor and vulnerable in society, becoming a true champion of his people.

LI JI
China
When a super-sized serpent began terrorizing locals and destroying crops, a young girl named Li Ji travelled up the mountain to kill it. As the slithering serpent prepared to attack, she plunged her sword into its neck and slayed it.

MAI AN TIÊM
Vietnam
Born enslaved, Mai An Tiêm rose through the ranks to become an official in the king's court. On one adventure, he came across an exotic-looking fruit. It was a watermelon, and he shared it with his people, who grew their own versions of this delicious fruit from its seeds.

BADANG
Malaysia
Life wasn't easy for Badang, who was born small and weak. His fortunes changed when a chance meeting with a water demon gave him formidable strength. Badang became a popular champion, defeating rival strongmen and helping people with difficult tasks, and word of his brawn spread far and wide.

HANDYONG
Philippines
There wasn't much that Handyong couldn't turn his hand to. He was as famous for his inventions as he was for destroying vicious monsters. He made the first boat, found ways to grow rice, and established a new set of local laws.

MINAMOTO NO YORIMITSU
Japan
A member of the Minamoto clan, Yorimitsu became a great samurai warrior, commander, and folk hero. With his team of four legendary swordsmen (see p.81), he defeated marauders and monsters in medieval Japan. His most famous escapade involved tackling a bloodthirsty oni (ogre) named Shuten-dōji. The severed head of the oni continued fighting Yorimitsu until our hero dealt the killer blow.

RATA
Tahiti
After his father was swallowed by a giant clam, the warrior prince Rata was set on revenge. He embarked on an epic ocean adventure, battling monsters and surviving storms in his quest for justice. Finally finding his father's remains, Rata brought him home for burial.

TUILAKEMBA
Fiji
Determined to find his absent father, Tuilakemba stormed into Skyland to challenge the celestial warriors. The god Tuilangi was so impressed he revealed that he was Tuilakemba's father. Brave Tuilakemba beat the evil gods and won lasting fame as a legendary warrior.

NART SASRYKVA
Caucasus region (Eastern Europe and Western Asia)
The ferocious fighter Nart achieved a never-ending list of famous feats during his lifetime. It included destroying a dragon, shooting down a star to use as a light, and stealing fire from deadly giants to benefit his brothers.

HAYK
Armenia
When the Babylonian king Bel threatened the warrior Hayk, this skilled archer shot his arrow and killed him outright. Then he took his 300 people far from home to Armenia. This heralded a new age of freedom and democracy as Hayk established his nation.

DOBRYNYA NIKITICH
Russia
Chaos ensued when a multiheaded dragon known as Zmey Gorynych captured the beloved niece of Prince Vladimir. The knight Dobrynya was the only man brave enough to come to the rescue. He killed the dragon and saved the girl.

IVAN TSAREVICH
Russia
When the tsar (emperor) asked his three sons to find out who was stealing his golden apples, the youngest, Ivan, discovered that the thief was the mythical firebird. He tracked it down, and the tsar rewarded his success by making him the heir to his kingdom.

SKUBA DRATEWKA
Poland
When an insatiable dragon started eating local girls, the king offered his daughter Wanda's hand in marriage to the man who could stop it. A clever shoemaker's apprentice named Skuba Dratewka killed the dragon with poison and married the princess.

LIBUŠE
Czechia
Wisdom and the power of prophecy made Libuše an exceptional ruler. But when her nation demanded a male leader, she put

her people first and stepped down from the throne. She later married the man who replaced her as the monarch, and together they founded the city of Prague.

TRIPTOLEMUS
Ancient Greece
The demigod Triptolemus earned the favour of Demeter, the goddess of agriculture. She shared all her farming knowledge, then gave him a winged chariot pulled by a serpent so he could travel the world helping people produce bountiful harvests.

PHORONEUS
Ancient Greece
Early Greeks lived without cities and laws until Zeus, king of the gods, made the demigod Phoroneus their first ruler. This hero united the people into one harmonious community, founded the city of Argos, gave them laws, and shared his skills of making fire and forging metal.

CADMUS
Ancient Greece
When his sister Europa went missing, the Phoenician prince Cadmus went on a dangerous journey to find her. He slayed a dragon along the way. When the goddess Athena told Cadmus to sow the dragon's teeth in the ground, they sprouted into an army of warriors. Cadmus then founded the great city of Thebes and became its king.

OEDIPUS
Ancient Greece
Raised in Corinth, Oedipus was devastated when a prophecy revealed he was destined to kill his father and marry his mother. He travelled to Thebes where he correctly answered the riddle of the evil Sphinx, ending its reign of terror. Oedipus was crowned king of Thebes, but he could not escape his destiny. Through no fault of his own, the prophecy came true, and the tragic hero fled into exile.

ANTIGONE
Ancient Greece
Daughter of Oedipus, Princess Antigone of Thebes was unwavering in her loyalty to her dead brother, Polynices. When King Creon banned his burial, she carried on regardless. Even though this act was punishable by execution, Antigone defied the king to honour her brother, a heroic act of loyalty.

TARCHON AND TYRRHENUS
Etruscan civilization (Italy)
Two ambitious brothers founded the Etruscan civilization and its league of 12 cities. Tyrrhenus gave his name to the Tyrrhenians, the Greek name for

the Etruscans. Tarchon went on to join forces with Aeneas, whose descendants founded Rome (see pp.12, 79).

SERVIUS TULLIUS
Ancient Rome
The son of an enslaved woman, Servius rose from humble beginnings to become a legendary king of Rome in the sixth century BCE. Under his rule, the city expanded in size, built protective city walls, and introduced reforms to help the poorest in society.

HORATIUS COCLES
Ancient Rome
The fearless warrior Horatius stood firm when Etruscan king Lars Porsena advanced with his army on the city of Rome in 509 BCE (see p.156). As the other soldiers fled in fear, Horatius stayed and guarded the bridge across the River Tiber. He proved too strong for the enemy, blocking their entry and writing his name in the history books.

ATTILA
Germany
The ruthless warrior Attila ruled the Huns in the 5th century CE and expanded their empire over a vast territory, uniting different tribes across Europe. His armies were feared for their archers mounted on horseback, and his military victories over the Roman Empire became legendary.

BLENDA
Sweden
Against all odds, the brave warrior Blenda led an uprising of hundreds of women against a mighty Danish army. They didn't expect to win a physical battle, so instead they plied the Danish soldiers with drink and slaughtered them in their sleep.

LAGERTHA
Scandinavia
The Viking shieldmaiden (female warrior) Lagertha proved more than a match for her husband Ragnar Lothbrok, a legendary Viking king in the 9th century CE (see p.26). Brave and ambitious, she won his heart when she came to his aid in battle, dressed in men's clothing. She also possessed supernatural powers, including the ability to fly.

SCÁTHACH
Ireland (Celtic people)
A fortified castle on a remote island was the secret location where the warrior Scáthach trained young soldiers. She taught them how to wield weapons, and many of them won glory on the battlefield, including the famous warrior Cú Chulainn (see pp.64–65, 94).

DEU-LA-DEU MARTINS
Portugal
In 1369, Deu-la-Deu managed to fool the Castilian army advancing on her town. When she hurled loaves of bread at them, the invading soldiers assumed the town had enough food to survive a long siege. The army backed off, leaving Deu-la-Deu as the town's hero.

KIVIUQ
Arctic region, North America (Inuit peoples)
There are many threats in the icy Arctic, and the Inuit hero Kiviuq confronted them head on. His weapon of choice, a harpoon, and his magical powers combined to ensure he survived against bears, giants, monsters, and evil spirits.

KUTOYIS
North America (Blackfoot people)
Legend goes that Kutoyis was born from the blood of an injured buffalo. He made it his life's work to go from village to village and rescue anyone who was treated unfairly. This freedom fighter helped hundreds of people escape cruelty and find safety.

ARROW BOY
North America (Cheyenne people)
Arrow Boy was born with magical powers. When his people faced a terrible famine, he used his gift to turn old buffalo bones into herds of buffalo that roamed the land again. Buffalo hunting provided Arrow Boy's people with the food and clothing they needed for their survival.

THROWN AWAY AND LODGE BOY
North America (Midwestern and Plains peoples)
Separated after their mother was murdered, the twin boys Thrown Away and Lodge Boy were eventually reunited with their father. Ignoring his warnings of danger, the heroic brothers set off to slay one evil monster after another.

PECOS BILL
US
As a child, Pecos fell out of his family's wagon and was raised by coyotes who taught him all kinds of survival skills. He grew up to be a courageous cowboy, leading a life of adventure, including riding cougars, wrestling monsters, lassoing tornadoes, and eating dynamite.

GLOSSARY

AFTERLIFE
A realm where a person's spirit or soul journeys to after death. *See also* Heaven, Underworld.

ANCESTOR
A person from whom someone is descended; in some cultures, ancestors are revered as wise spirits and guides.

ASTROLOGER
Someone who uses the position of celestial objects, such as stars, to predict the future.

ATONE
Make amends.

BESIEGED
Surrounded by armed forces.

CELTIC
Relating to the Celts – a group of ancient peoples from Central Europe who spread to Ireland, Britain, and parts of France and Spain.

CHIVALRY
The qualities expected of an ideal knight, such as courage, honour, courtesy, and good manners towards women.

CLAN
A group of families or people with shared ancestors.

COAT OF ARMS
A set of heraldic symbols used by a noble family.

CULTURE
Shared beliefs, customs, and way of life unique to a specific group of people.

DEITY
An immortal, powerful being worshipped by others. A god.

DEMIGOD
In some cultures, a being that has one divine parent and one human parent.

DEMON
An evil spirit that torments people and causes pain and suffering.

DYNASTY
A family or group ruling a region for successive generations.

ENSLAVEMENT
Making someone a slave – claiming to own them and their labour.

EPIC
A long narrative poem, describing the adventures of a heroic person or the exploits of a nation.

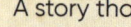

FAIRYTALE
A story that often features mythical creatures and magic. Fairy tales may have a moral or cautionary message.

FOLKLORE
Traditional beliefs and stories that have been passed on for many years, commonly by word of mouth.

HEAVEN
In some cultures, a place above the sky that is believed to be the home of the gods, or a place where the spirits of good people go after death.

IMMORTAL
A being that can live for ever.

INDIGENOUS
A person or group of people that come from a particular place, and have lived there since the earliest times.

KNIGHT
In medieval Europe, a warrior who swore loyalty to a monarch or another noble, followed a code of chivalry, and fought for them on horseback.

LABOURS
Challenging tasks undertaken by a hero.

LEGEND
A story of a famous deed from the past that is retold by many but cannot be proved. Some legends have sprung up as recently as the 19th century, and some involve long-ago people or events that may have a historical basis.

MAGIC
A mysterious, supernatural force.
Magic can be naturally possessed
by beings or objects, or used to
cast spells or curses.

MEDIEVAL
From a period of history in
Europe, also called the Middle
Ages, between the 5th and
15th centuries CE.

MINSTREL
A medieval entertainer, who sang
songs and recited poetry.

MORTAL
A being that will die one day.

MYTH
A story used by early peoples
to explain the world around them.

MYTHOLOGY
A people or culture's collection
of related myths. Also refers to
the study of myths.

NORSE
From ancient and medieval Norway
or Scandinavia. Vikings were Norse
people who flourished from the 8th
to 11th centuries CE.

ORAL
Passed on by word of mouth.

PHARAOH
A ruler in ancient Egypt.

POLYNESIA
An area of Oceania, made up
of more than 1,000 small islands.

QUEST
A journey made with a particular
goal, or in search of something; it
is often long and difficult.

REALM
Another word for kingdom, or an
area controlled by a ruler. It can
also be an otherworldly space
that can be reached through
magic or time travel.

SACRED
Connected with a god, and
considered holy and worthy
of respect.

SHAMAN
In some cultures, a person who can
communicate with an invisible spirit
world, using magic and chants.

SHAPESHIFT
To transform from one physical
form to another.

SLAVIC
Relating to the Slavs – a group
of people from northern Eurasia,
including Russia, Belarus, Ukraine,
Poland, and the Balkans.

SORCERER
A person who practises magic.

TITAN
In Greek mythology, the first gods
to rule the world, before the gods of
Mount Olympus.

TRIALS
A series of challenges that
test a person's strength and
determination; these challenges
may be life-threatening.

TRICKSTER
A mischievous being who upsets
deities and the normal order of
things. Some tricksters outwit
their foes to perform heroic deeds.

TYRANT
A ruler who has unlimited power over
their people, and uses it cruelly.

UNDERWORLD
In some cultures, the land or realm
of the dead.

INDEX

Page numbers in **bold** show featured heroes.

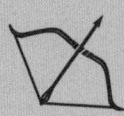

ACKNOWLEDGMENTS

Dorling Kindersley would like to thank the following people for their help with making the book:
Vandana Likhmania, Pranay Mathur, Lizzie Munsey, Soumya Rampal, Rupa Rao, Neha Ruth Samuel, and Janashree Singha for editorial assistance; Revati Anand for design assistance; Dheeraj Arora for jacket finishes; Lisa Jane Gillespie and the DK Inclusion and Impact Team for a sensitivity check; Geetam Biswas, Shubhdeep Kaur, Rituraj, and Ridhima Sikka for picture research assistance, and Manpreet Kaur for picture research administration support; Carron Brown for proofreading; and Elizabeth Wise for indexing.

Contributors and consultants:

Andrea Mills is an award-winning author of more than 70 fiction and reference book titles for children of all ages.

Lizzie Munsey writes and edits books for children. She has worked in publishing for more than a decade, and has contributed to scores of books on a wide range of subjects, including space, science, natural history, geography, history, and maths.

Nathan Robert Brown is an author and mythologist known for his written works about folklore, urban legends, and ancient myths, making old tales accessible to modern audiences.

Sarosh Arif is an award-winning educator, author, and internationally recognized editorial and history consultant.

Steve Hoffman is a freelance contributor and consultant specializing in non-fiction books for children.

Dr Pearl K Brower, Iñupiaq, is the President/CEO of Ukpeaġvik Iñupiat Corporation.

Dr Manuel May Castillo is a Mayan Indigenous scholar from Mexico who specializes in heritage and socio-cultural anthropology. He is a Program Manager at the Smithsonian NMAI.

Dr Mary-Alice Daniel is the author of two books exploring African storytelling traditions and an Associate Research Scholar at Princeton University, where she teaches a signature seminar on African Mythology and Narratology.

Dr Pavel Horák is a scholar based in Austria and Czechia. His research focuses on paganism, esotericism, magic, and heritage studies.

Aziza Ibrokhimova is the Head of the Tourism Department at the State Museum of the History of Uzbekistan. She is passionate about cultural preservation and education, and making history and heritage more accessible to young audiences.

Salima Ikram is a Distinguished University Professor at The American University in Cairo. She has directed several archaeological and museological projects in Egypt, and publishes in both scholarly and popular venues.

Carolyne Larrington is a retired professor in medieval literature at the University of Oxford. She researches mythology and legend, with a particular interest in women.

Dr Ragnhild Ljosland is a lecturer at the University of the Highlands and Islands (Scotland), specializing in culture and heritage, Runology, and Scandinavian and Scottish sociolinguistics.

Andrew Hock Soon Ng is an Associate Professor at Monash University Malaysia, where he researches on Asian folktales and Gothic horror, and teaches creative writing and literary studies.

Hammad Rind is a multilingual writer and translator. His debut novel, *Four Dervishes* (2021), blends satire and magic realism, drawing inspiration from classical literature.

David Stuttard is a classicist, historian, dramatist, and author of numerous books about the ancient Greeks and Romans, including their mythology.

Timothy Topper (Cheyenne River Sioux), MEd, EdD, is a student affairs practitioner working at colleges and universities in the US, focusing on Indigenous futurism and advocacy.

Stock Photo: Peter Horree (tl). Shutterstock.com: NDK Studio (c); SachyStd (tc). 29 Alamy Stock Photo: The History Collection (tl); Well / BOT. Shutterstock.com: NDK Studio (cl). 30 © The Trustees of the British Museum. All rights reserved: (cl). Shutterstock.com: designersayma97 (tl). 30–31 Getty Images: Pictures from History / Universal Images Group. 31 Shutterstock.com: j_fredz (br); NDK Studio (bl). 32 Bridgeman Images: (tl); © Look and Learn (br). 33 Alamy Stock Photo: © Fine Art Images / Heritage Images (t). Photo Scala, Florence: Foto Smithsonian American Art Museum / Art Resource (b). Shutterstock.com: MonikaJ (cl). 34 Alamy Stock Photo: Cinematic Collection / TOUCHSTONE (bc). Bridgeman Images: National Museums & Galleries of Wales (bl). Dreamstime.com: Vectaray (crb). Shutterstock.com: Cosmic_Design (tl); Mansell Collection / The LIFE Picture Collection (tr). 35 Alamy Stock Photo: dpa picture alliance. 37 Depositphotos Inc: MioBuono12 (tr). 38 Getty Images: Historical Picture Archive / Corbis (b). 39 Alamy Stock Photo: GRANGER - Historical Picture Archive (c); NMUIM (br). Shutterstock.com: NDK Studio (tr). 40–41 Adobe Stock: nenk123 (bc). Dreamstime.com: Andrii Naumenko. 40 Adobe Stock: Dmitriy Vlasov (tr). Depositphotos Inc: rudall30 (bl). Dreamstime.com: Svetlana Alyuk (c); Yevgenii Movliev (tl). Getty Images / iStock: ambassador806 (bc). Shutterstock.com: Wiliarta (tc). 41 Dreamstime.com: Yevgenii Movliev (tr). Shutterstock.com: vectorisland (cl). 42 Bridgeman Images: © Look and Learn. 43 Alamy Stock Photo: Tibbut Archive (br); United Archives GmbH / Carl Simon (tr). Dreamstime.com: Vectaray (bl). Heidelberg University Library: (c). 44 Bridgeman Images: © Archives Charmet (t); © Iberfoto (br). Dreamstime.com: Svetlana Alyuk (clb). Shutterstock.com: NDK Studio (cr). 45 Depositphotos Inc: rudall30 (tl). Dreamstime.com: Timurk (br). The J. Paul Getty Museum, Los Angeles: (cl). 46 Alamy Stock Photo: Penta Springs Limited / Artokoloro (cl); Pictorial Press Ltd (tr). Shutterstock.com: NDK Studio (tc). 46–47 Alamy Stock Photo: H-AB. 47 Shutterstock.com: SNicky (tl). 52 Buddha's crystal and other fairy stories: Yei Theodora Ozaki. 53 Alamy Stock Photo: Lebrecht Music & Arts / Music-Images (b). Shutterstock.com: Wiliarta (tc). 54 Alamy Stock Photo: Dinodia Photos (tr); Eraza Collection (bl). Getty Images: Stefano Bianchetti / Corbis (bc); Hulton Archive / Historica Graphica Collection / Heritage Images (br). Mission Pavie en Indochine: (cla). 55 Alamy Stock Photo: Lakeview Images (br). Depositphotos Inc: MioBuono12 (bl). Getty Images: Sepia Times / Universal Images Group (tc). 56 Buddy Whitethorne Foundation: artwork by Baje Whitethorne Sr.. Dreamstime.com: Vivilweb (tr); Yodke67 (tl). 57 Alamy Stock Photo: Science History Images. Dreamstime.com: Vladimir Yudin (ca). Shutterstock.com: NDK Studio (clb). 58 Dreamstime.com: Jonatan Stockton (cla). 58–59 Bridgeman Images: Christie's Images. 59 Getty Images / iStock: ambassador806 (tl). 60

Shutterstock.com: NDK Studio (cra). 62 Alamy Stock Photo: Science History Images / Photo Researchers (b). The J. Paul Getty Museum, Los Angeles: (tr). 63 Getty Images: AFP / Issouf Sanogo / Staff (bl). Shutterstock.com: NDK Studio (cl). 64 Alamy Stock Photo: Visual Arts Resource. 65 Alamy Stock Photo: Chronicle (cl); Neil G Paterson (bl). Dreamstime.com: Christos Georghiou (tl). Whyte's: (r). 66 Alamy Stock Photo: Adam Eastland (cl); VTR (cb). © The Trustees of the British Museum. All rights reserved: (tr). Depositphotos Inc: MioBuono12 (ca). The Metropolitan Museum of Art: Rogers Fund, 1910 (cr). 67 Alamy Stock Photo: Album (tl). Angela Babby: (r). Getty Images: De Agostini / DEA / A. De Gregorio (cl). 68 Adobe Stock: Enola99d (tl). Alamy Stock Photo: The Picture Art Collection (cl). Bridgeman Images: Lebrecht History. Shutterstock.com: NDK Studio (br). 69 Adobe Stock: Vikivector (tl). Alamy Stock Photo: Niday Picture Library (cl). 70–71 Queensland Art Gallery | Gallery of Modern Art (QAGOMA). 71 Alamy Stock Photo: GL Archive (tr); The Picture Art Collection (tl). Shutterstock.com: NDK Studio (crb). 72 Shutterstock.com: NDK Studio (cr). 74 Alamy Stock Photo: Keith Corrigan (tr); Private Collection / AF Fotografie (b). Shutterstock.com: Artur. B (tl). 75 Alamy Stock Photo: LLP collection. Shutterstock.com: Taawon Graphics (tl). 77 Adobe Stock: Mamun360 (tc). 78 Alamy Stock Photo: Ivan Vdovin. Dreamstime.com: Kitekit (tl). Shutterstock.com: NDK Studio (tc). 79 Alamy Stock Photo: incamerastock (cr). The Metropolitan Museum of Art: The Friedsam Collection, Bequest of Michael Friedsam, 1931. Shutterstock.com: MonikaJ (clb); Park Ji Sun (tc). 80–81 Bridgeman Images: © Mead Art Museum / Gift of William Green. 81 Alamy Stock Photo: amana images inc. (ca); Penta Springs Limited / Artokoloro (br). Getty Images: The Asahi Shimbun (tr). Shutterstock.com: NDK Studio (tc). 82 Dreamstime.com: Vakabungo (tc). Getty Images: V. Muthuraman / IndiaPictures / Universal Images Group (cr). 82–83 Alamy Stock Photo: The Picture Art Collection (b). 83 Alamy Stock Photo: Art Collection 2 (tr). 84–85 Alamy Stock Photo: The Picture Art Collection (texture). Dreamstime.com: Katemykate. 86 Getty Images / iStock: DigitalVision Vectors / AlonzoDesign (tc). Shutterstock.com: EvijaF (bl); NDK Studio (tl). 87 Alamy Stock Photo: Pictures Now (t). Dreamstime.com: Ddgrigg (clb). Shutterstock.com: NDK Studio (br). 88–89 Alamy Stock Photo: Penta Springs Limited / Artokoloro. 88 Okayama Prefectural Museum: (tl). 89 Alamy Stock Photo: GRANGER - Historical Picture Archive (br). Dreamstime.com: Farrukh Maqbool (tc). Shutterstock.com: NDK Studio (crb). 90 Adobe Stock: nenk123 (tc). Xuân-Lam Nguyn. Shutterstock.com: NDK Studio (cr). 91 Alamy Stock Photo: Arterra Picture Library / Clement Philippe (tr). Getty Images / iStock: hansgertbroeder (b). Shutterstock.com: Vlad Ra27 (tl). 92 Alamy Stock Photo: Alexander Mitrofanov (br). Dreamstime.com: Lina Budiarti (tc). Shutterstock.com: Syahtuah Mohamed (l);

MonikaJ (cr). 93 Coronari Auctions. 94 Alamy Stock Photo: Visual Arts Resource (bl). Dreamstime.com: Saiko3p (c); Jozef Sedmak (tl); Vectaray (br). 95 Alamy Stock Photo: North Wind Picture Archives0 (cl); Well / BOT (bl); Pictorial Press (bc). © The Trustees of the British Museum. All rights reserved: (br). Getty Images / iStock: Anutr Tosirikul (tr). 96 Depositphotos Inc: MioBuono12 (cl). 97 Alamy Stock Photo: PhotoStock-Israel / Historic Illustrations (tl); Science History Images / Photo Researchers (r). 98 Dreamstime.com: Kobby Dagan (crb). Shutterstock.com: NDK Studio (cl). Vibal Group, Inc: Ferdinand Doctolero. 99 Alamy Stock Photo: History and Art Collection (b). Dreamstime.com: Enal Agustin (tc). 100 Alamy Stock Photo: Historic Collection (b). Dreamstime.com: Oleksandr Melnyk (tl). 101 Mission Pavie en Indochine. 102 Shutterstock.com: Bulgn (br). 103 Alamy Stock Photo: Album (br); Albert Seligman (tr). 104 Adobe Stock: Olinotila (tl). 104–105 Bridgeman Images: Ghigo Roli (b). 105 Alamy Stock Photo: Mouseion Archives (tr); Konrad Zelazowski (tl). 107 Dreamstime.com: Vectaray (tl). 110 Toit Te Whenua - Land Information New Zealand: Kupe fighting Te Wheke, Cliff Whiting (1990). Reproduced with permission of Ngā Pou Taunaha o Aotearoa New Zealand Geographic Board. Crown Copyright Reserved. 111 Toit Te Whenua - Land Information New Zealand: Paikea, Cliff Whiting (1990). Reproduced with permission of Ngā Pou Taunaha o Aotearoa New Zealand Geographic Board. Crown Copyright Reserved. 112–113 Getty Images: De Agostini / DEA / A. DAGLI ORTI. 112 Alamy Stock Photo: Smith Archive (cl). Shutterstock.com: MonikaJ (bl); Jorge Ural (tl). 113 Alamy Stock Photo: Charles Walker Collection (tr). Bridgeman Images: Photo © North Wind Pictures (br). 114–115 © The Trustees of the British Museum. All rights reserved. 114 Alamy Stock Photo: mauritius images GmbH / Steve Vidler (br). Getty Images: Sepia Times / Universal Images Group (bl). Shutterstock.com: NDK Studio (cl). 116 Alamy Stock Photo: Albert Seligman (tr); World History Archive (bl). Bridgeman Images: Collection Gregoire (br). Dreamstime.com: Vectaray (cb). Shutterstock.com: Bulgn (tl). 117 Photo Scala, Florence: Christie's Images, London. 118 Dreamstime.com: Vectaray (bl). 120 Alamy Stock Photo: Jimlop collection. Dreamstime.com: Lainspiratriz Inspiratriz (tc). Shutterstock.com: MonikaJ (cb). 121 Dreamstime.com: Oleksandr Kovernik (tl). Getty Images: De Agostini / DEA / G. SIOEN (tr); DEA / A. DAGLI ORTI / De Agostini (b). 122 Alamy Stock Photo: Album (br); Well / BOT (tr). Dreamstime.com: Arturoosorno. 123 Alamy Stock Photo: Artepics (tr); BTEU / RKM (cl). Bridgeman Images: From the British Library archive (c); © Look and Learn (cr). 124–125 Alamy Stock Photo: Zuri Swimmer. 125 Alamy Stock Photo: ARTGEN (cl); Mikhail Olykaynen (crb). Bridgeman Images: (tr). Dreamstime.com: Vectaray (cb); Ylivdesign (tl). 126 Alamy Stock Photo: Maidun Collection. Dreamstime.com: Anastasiia Sklyarova (tl). Shutterstock.com:

NDK Studio (clb). **127 Alamy Stock Photo:** © Fine Art Images / Heritage Images (cla); Zuri Swimmer (b). **128–129 Bridgeman Images:** Photograph © 2025 Museum of Fine Arts, Boston. All rights reserved. / Gift of Landon T. Clay. **128 Bridgeman Images:** Museum of Fine Arts, Houston / Gift of Frank Carroll in memory of Frank and Eleanor Carroll (bl). **Shutterstock. com:** Eroshka (cb). **129 Alamy Stock Photo:** David Sanger Photography (bc). **Bridgeman Images:** Photograph © 2025 Museum of Fine Arts, Boston. All rights reserved. / William Francis Warden Fund (bl). **Getty Images:** Myloupe / Universal Images Group (cb). **130 Alamy Stock Photo:** Ivy Close Images (br). **© The Trustees of the British Museum. All rights reserved:** (t). **131 Alamy Stock Photo:** History and Art Collection (t). **132 123RF.com:** matriyoshka (tl). **Dreamstime.com:** Patrick Guenette (cra). **Getty Images / iStock:** Vetta / CSA Images (br). **133 Adobe Stock:** Alice (bl). **Alamy Stock Photo:** Pictorial Press Ltd (cb); Adebayo Salawu (br). **Shutterstock.com:** bee enk (bc). **134 Volcano Art Center:** Maui Snaring The Sun, by Dietrich Varez.. **135 123RF. com:** buravtsoff123 (cla). **Dreamstime.com:** Vectaray (cl). **Te Whare o Rehua Sarjeant Gallery:** E. Mervyn Taylor 'Maui and Mahuika circa 1944-1964, colour linocut on paper, 1982/24/2. Collection of Te Whare o Rehua Sarjeant Gallery, Whanganui, New Zealand. Gift of Sir John Te Herekiekie Grace, Whanganui, 1982. (tr). **Volcano Art Center:** Maui Lifting The Sky, by Dietrich Varez (b). **136–137 The Algonquin legends of New England. 136 Adobe Stock:** MicroOne (ca). **Alamy Stock Photo:** Cultural Archive (cla). **Depositphotos Inc:** MioBuono12 (crb). **137 Dreamstime.com:** Rixie (tl). **David Wong:** (r). **138 Alamy Stock Photo:** Alexander Mitrofanov (bl); The Picture Art Collection (tr). **139 Alamy Stock Photo:** Images & Stories. **Shutterstock.com:** NDK Studio (cra). **140 Alamy Stock Photo:** Pictorial Press Ltd. **141 Getty Images / iStock:** Amin Nur Rochman (clb). **National Library of Poland (Biblioteka Narodowa, Warszawa). 142 Alamy Stock Photo:** Ville Eek (bl). **Depositphotos Inc:** MioBuono12 (tl). **142–143 Alamy Stock Photo:** LMA / AW. **143 Dreamstime.com:** TOPVECTORSTOCK (tl). **Getty Images:** DeAgostini (tr). **Momotaro:** (cr). **144 Bridgeman Images:** G. Dagli Orti / © NPL - DeA Picture Library (bl); © Look and Learn (t). **Ronan McCormick:** (br). **145 Alamy Stock Photo:** Zuri Swimmer (bl). **Depositphotos Inc:** MioBuono12 (cr). **Dreamstime.com:** Wirestock (tl). **Image Courtesy: Panjab Digital Library:** (bc). **Xuân-Lam Nguyn:** (tr). **146 Alamy Stock Photo:** GRANGER - Historical Picture Archive. **Dreamstime.com:** Vitaly Ilyasov (ca). **Shutterstock.com:** NDK Studio (tr). **146–147 Shutterstock.com:** Nataliia K. **147 Alamy Stock Photo:** Ivy Close Images; Penta Springs Limited / Artokoloro (tl). **148 Shutterstock.com:** Alexander_P (tl). **149 Depositphotos Inc:** MioBuono12 (cl). **The Orange Fairy Tale Book. 150 Dreamstime.com:** Barmaleeva (tc); Vectaray (cla). **150–151 Robin McNeal. 151**

Alamy Stock Photo: Paul Brown (tr). **Getty Images:** Pictures From History / Universal Images Group (tl). **152 Alamy Stock Photo:** Omoniyi Ayedun Olubunmi (cr); Adebayo Salawu. **Dreamstime.com:** Vectaray (br). **153 Alamy Stock Photo:** Yurii Moroz. **Dreamstime. com:** Vectaray (br). **Shutterstock.com:** bee enk (clb). **154 Depositphotos Inc:** MioBuono12 (cl). **Dreamstime.com:** Lesia Pavlenko (tl). **Getty Images:** Moment / Alex Saurel. **155 Bridgeman Images:** Photo © The Holbarn Archive (br). **Dreamstime.com:** Patrick Guenette (clb). **STUDIO WILLEN GMBH:** Landesmuseum Zurich (t). **156 Adobe Stock:** Alice (cb). **Bridgeman Images:** © Giuseppe Rava. All Rights Reserved 2025 (bl). **Los Angeles County Museum of Art:** Giulio di Antonio Bonasone (Italy, Bologna, circa 1498-1580) (t). **157 Adobe Stock:** Extremus (clb). **Dreamstime.com:** Ssstocker (tl). **Image Courtesy: Panjab Digital Library:** (r). **158 Bridgeman Images:** © Look and Learn. **159 Adobe Stock:** Meth Mehr (tl). **Shutterstock.com:** NDK Studio (c). **Tatra Gallery, Poprad:** (tr). **University of Delaware:** Museums Collections, University of Delaware, Gift of the Continental American Life Insurance Company, 1944 / Artist- Newell Convers Wyeth (b). **160 Alamy Stock Photo:** Historical Art Collection (HAC) (tc). **R. Michelson Galleries:** Sheldon Fogelman Agency, Inc.. **Shutterstock.com:** NDK Studio (clb). **161 Lisa Boyur. Depositphotos Inc:** MioBuono12 (br). **Dreamstime.com:** Cobectbhax (clb). **162 Dreamstime.com:** Evgeniy Kuznetsov (tc); Vectaray (cl). **Getty Images:** Hannah Foslien / Stringer (cr). **Getty Images / iStock:** Vetta / CSA Images (tl). **Library of Congress, Washington, D.C.:** LC-USZ62-43513 / Correll, Richard V (b). **163 Getty Images / iStock:** PictureLake. **164 Adobe Stock:** sudevi (tr). **Dreamstime.com:** Ievgen Melamud (tc); Tech Zaka (br). **Shutterstock.com:** Gluiki (bl). **165 Dreamstime.com:** Robert Adrian Hillman (ca); Natbasil (tc); Anastasia Maslova (tl). **Getty Images / iStock:** BJarts (cra). **166 Llyfrgell Genedlaethol Cymru – The National Library of Wales:** with permission from the Margaret Dorothy Jones family. **167 The Cleveland Museum Of Art:** Leonard C. Hanna Jr. Fund 1991.1 (t). **168–169 Photograph © 2024 Museum of Fine Arts, Boston. 168 Dreamstime. com:** Anastasia Maslova (tl). **Shutterstock.com:** MonikaJ (tr). **169 Shutterstock.com:** MonikaJ (cl). **170 Alamy Stock Photo:** Jim West (cl). **Depositphotos Inc:** MioBuono12 (cr). **171 Alamy Stock Photo:** CPA Media Pte Ltd / Pictures From History (cl); Armands Pharyos (br). **172 Bridgeman Images:** Photo © The Holbarn Archive (tl). **Dreamstime.com:** Alexstar (br); Tech Zaka (tc). **Shutterstock.com:** NDK Studio (cr). **173 Bridgeman Images:** Photo © The Holbarn Archive (tl). **The Metropolitan Museum of Art:** The Grinnell Collection, Bequest of William Milne Grinnell, 1920 (br). **174 Alamy Stock Photo:** Ivy Close Images (tr). **Dreamstime.com:** Vectaray (tc). **Getty Images:** Sepia Times / Universal Images Group. **175 Alamy Stock Photo:** incamerastock / ICP (cla). **Dreamstime. com:** Timurk (bl). **Essentiel Galerie SRL:** (br).

Volcano Art Center: Mānaiakalani (Māuis Fishhook), by Catherine Wynne (bc). **176 Bridgeman Images:** Photo © The Holbarn Archive (tl). **Dreamstime.com:** Vectaray (cr). **Getty Images / iStock:** BJarts (tc). **177 Cyrillius. Dreamstime.com:** Alexey Arzamastsev (bl); Ievgen Melamud (tl). **178 Alamy Stock Photo:** Artepics (b). **Shutterstock.com:** Moleng24 (tl). **TopFoto:** Fortean (tr). **179 akg-images:** Fototeca Gilardi. **Dreamstime.com:** Wektorygrafika (tl). **Shutterstock.com:** NDK Studio (c). **180 Bridgeman Images:** © Look and Learn; Photo © CCI (tl). **181 Dreamstime.com:** Natbasil (tl); Vectaray (crb). **Shutterstock.com:** WILLIAM RG (clb). **186 123RF. com:** buravtsoff123 (bl). **Adobe Stock:** Olinotila (fcrb). **Alamy Stock Photo:** amana images inc. (bc). **Dreamstime.com:** Christos Georghiou (fbl); Tech Zaka (clb); Vakabungo (bl/Bow); Zag4x4 (br). **Shutterstock.com:** Bulgn (crb); Taawon Graphics (fbl/warrior). **187 Dreamstime.com:** Svetlana Alyuk (fbl); Serhii Borodin (bc). **Getty Images / iStock:** ambassador806 (clb). **Shutterstock.com:** Cosmic_Design (bl); designersayma97 (crb); Jorge Ural (br/sacred). **188 Adobe Stock:** Alice (bc/Aphrodite). **Alamy Stock Photo:** Pictorial Press Ltd (fbl). **Dreamstime.com:** Ddgrigg (fbr/Green); Ylivdesign (bl/Kantele); Vitaly Ilyasov (fbl/Samurai); Oleksandr Kovernik (bc/lyre); Kitekit (br/arrows); Evgeniy Kuznetsov (fbr/bull); Yodke67 (fbr/feather). **189 Adobe Stock:** Enola99d (fbl); Mamun360 (bc/Viking); nenk123 (bl/Big). **Dreamstime.com:** Enal Agustin (br/Archer); Kitekit (bl, crb/feathers); Evgeniy Kuznetsov (br); Lesia Pavlenko (fbr); Ssstocker (cb)

Cover images: *Front and Back:* **Getty Images / iStock:** littleclie; *Front:* **Getty Images:** Hulton Archive / Heritage Art / Heritage Images b; **Getty Images / iStock:** sergio34 ca; *Back:* **Alamy Stock Photo:** Tony Mcnicol cb, Pictorial Press bl, Science History Images / Photo Researchers tl, Albert Seligman tr, The Picture Art Collection br; *Spine:* **Alamy Stock Photo:** David Sanger Photography c.